ROAD RESEARCH

research on
traffic corridor control

**A REPORT PREPARED
BY AN OECD ROAD RESEARCH GROUP**

NOVEMBER 1975

ORGANISATION FOR ECONOMIC CO-OPERATION AND DEVELOPMENT

The Organisation for Economic Co-operation and Development (OECD) was set up under a Convention signed in Paris on 14th December, 1960, which provides that the OECD shall promote policies designed :
— to achieve the highest sustainable economic growth and employment and a rising standard of living in Member countries, while maintaining financial stability, and thus to contribute to the development of the world economy;
— to contribute to sound economic expansion in Member as well as non-member countries in the process of economic development;
— to contribute to the expansion of world trade on a multilateral, non-discriminatory basis in accordance with international obligations.

The Members of OECD are Australia, Austria, Belgium, Canada, Denmark, Finland, France, the Federal Republic of Germany, Greece, Iceland, Ireland, Italy, Japan, Luxembourg, the Netherlands, New Zealand, Norway, Portugal, Spain, Sweden, Switzerland, Turkey, the United Kingdom and the United States.

*
* *

FOREWORD

The Road Research Programme has two main fields of activity:
- promotion of international co-operation in road construction, safety and traffic, the co-ordination of research facilities available in Member countries and the scientific interpretation of the results of joint experiments;
- International Road Research Documentation, a co-operative scheme for the systematic exchange of information on scientific literature and of current research programmes in Member countries.

The present programme is primarily concerned with defining the scientific and technological basis needed to assist governments of Member countries in decision-making on the most urgent road problems:
- planning, design and maintenance of the total road infrastructure, taking account of economic, social and technical developments and needs;
- formulation, planning and implementation of common overall strategies for road safety;
- improvement of traffic control systems, both in urban and in rural areas, to optimise traffic operation and to enhance quality of service provided to road users;
- development and evaluation of integrated urban and suburban transport strategies, taking into account economic, social, energy and environmental requirements.

*

* *

The Group "International Corridor Experiment" (ICE-Project) was created to examine the strategies available for traffic corridor control and to outline potential international co-ordinated research that could be performed on a corridor facility of a Member country on the basis of the needs of another Member country. The ICE-Project has been a prime example of co-operative research into the intricate problems of effective traffic control systems by electronic aids to ease traffic flow, prevent accidents, minimise environmental effects and contribute to energy conservation. It has enabled a large consortium of Member countries to pool their efforts and share the cost of development work. The following report, a result of the activities and meetings held in Europe, Japan and the United States, between 1971 and 1974, presents a first international review of the state-of-the-art in this field. The findings and conclusions of the Group as well as the research efforts initiated should help to validate and further develop present traffic corridor control concepts.

PREFACE

The advantage of traffic corridor control especially of co-ordinating city and motorway traffic in a corridor lies in the optimum utilisation of existing traffic facilities. This advantage is even more significant when viewed in light of the increasing demand upon urban transport facilities and increasing difficulties related to the provision of new urban motorways. The underlying aim of this Road Research Group, the "International Corridor Experiment", was to examine the strategies available for the most efficient operation of different types of motorway corridors and to outline potential studies and/or experiments that could be performed on a facility of a Member country on the basis of the research needs of another Member country. Underlying this aim was the intention to bring together and to exploit the expertise in traffic control available in participating OECD countries in order to make the most rapid and efficient impact on the very complex subject of traffic corridor control.

The Group identified the basic objective of traffic corridor control as the improvement of overall cost effectiveness through optimising the utilisation of the road network within the corridor. The costs involved include the direct costs to the road user, both local and through traffic (e.g. accidents, journey times, fuel consumption, unexpected delay, irritation and discomfort of drivers) and the indirect costs to the residents within or adjacent to the corridor (e.g. air pollution, noise, vibration and some of the effects of accidents). The criteria for corridor control may differ depending on local traffic conditions and control policy and furthermore the priority of objectives is a matter of local or national policy decisions.

Corridor control systems vary according to the physical facilities included within the corridor and according to the control strategy adopted. The Group examined the nature of the various systems and strategies and inventoried existing corridor facilities. A primary result of the Group's efforts in this phase of work is a comprehensive state-of-the-art of traffic corridor control concepts.

Assessment procedures are necessary in order to monitor the operation and efficiency of the traffic corridor control system that has been implemented in order to determine whether or not the system objectives have been met. An assessment methodology was set forth by the Group which includes the evaluation of the problems, the analysis of solutions and the documentation of results. The Group concluded that there exists a high priority need for methods designed to evaluate the various types of corridor control, ranging from methods for testing various control strategies to the development of cost-benefit analysis techniques.

The major aspects of economic analysis of corridor traffic control systems were outlined by the Group. However, it was pointed out that since corridor control constituted an advanced traffic engineering technique, experimental projects may be implemented for other reasons than those merely concerned with concrete economic accountability. Moreover, it was emphasized that there is considerable difficulty in assigning monetary values to many of the anticipated results listed in the corridor control goals.

The report of the Group provides road administrators and road traffic engineers with a state-of-the-art review of a valuable tool for alleviating traffic congestion. The Group has concluded that, as more research is completed in this area, the assessment of traffic corridor problems and their potential solutions will be more reliable. Finally, the significance of the work of this Group should not be measured only in terms of the results of the co-operative projects, but in terms of having established a new tool for international co-operative road transport research. This new tool consists of sharing not only research results, but actually undertaking research on a joint international basis.

TABLE OF CONTENTS

I

INTRODUCTION

I.1 Background

The first triennial (1968-1970) OECD programme of co-operation in road research, in particular the Road Research Groups which prepared the reports, Area Traffic Control Systems and Electronic Aids for Freeway Operations(1), yielded the recommendation of the problem of co-ordinating city and motorway traffic as an outstanding subject for future co-operative research. Consequently, a multilateral research project designated Road Research Group, "International Corridor Experiment (ICE)", was integrated in 1971 by the Steering Committee for Road Research as part of the OECD Road Research Programme.

The purpose of this collaboration was to bring together and exploit the expertise in traffic control available in participating OECD countries in order to make the most rapid and efficient impact on the very complex subject of traffic corridor control. The experience of developments such as ramp control systems in the United States, co-ordinated signal control in Europe, and motorist warning systems in Japan provided the basis for the Group's work. The underlying aim of the ICE-Project was to examine the strategies available for the most efficient operation of different types of motorway corridors and to outline potential studies and/or experiments that could be performed on a facility of a Member country on the basis of the research needs of another Member country. Inherent in this aim is the recognition that international co-operation can help greatly to make the optimum use of scarce research funds, to advance the present state-of-the-art and to promote the formation of internationally accepted standardized traffic controls and measures.

The Road Research Group co-ordinated its efforts with the European Economic Community/COST Project 30 Study Group which has the same broad research area, but which concentrated on hardware aspects of methods of communication with the driver, whereas the OECD Group focused their work on strategies (software) for corridor traffic control. This division of work corresponds to the requirements of OECD countries to advance progress in the field of strategic control modes which could be readily applied to the various types of corridor facilities, and reflects the specific needs of European countries for the development of a standard method of communication with drivers. The research results obtained by both groups will be made available to Member countries participating in either OECD or COST.

I.2 Scope of Study

The following five types of corridors, both in urban and in rural areas (intra-city and inter-city), were considered within the framework of the programme:

1. Motorway and motorway;
2. Motorway and co-ordinated area traffic control system;

---

1) See list of publications at the end of this report.

3. Motorway and street network (unco-ordinated control);

4. Motorway and suburban road network (including controlled arterials);

5. Motorway and rural roads.

The control strategies for corridor types 2, 3 and 4 may include parking control. The special control of bus and truck traffic within a traffic corridor was considered as part of the overall traffic corridor problem. The optimisation of mass transit in general, within the boundaries of a traffic corridor, was not included in the Group's field of interest. The problem of communication to drivers was included insofar as it is of importance for the control of traffic corridors.

I.3 Accomplishments

During the course of its meetings held between 1971 and 1974 in Europe, Japan and the United States, the Group accomplished the following:

1. prepared a statement of the goals and objectives of traffic corridor control (Chapter II);

2. examined the nature of various corridor control systems, reviewed the state-of-the-art in certain key problem areas, and inventoried existing corridor facilities (Chapter III and Annexes 2 through 7);

3. examined the evaluative criteria for the assessment of corridor traffic control systems (Chapter IV);

4. examined the major aspects of economic analysis of corridor traffic control systems (Chapter V);

5. identified the research needs in corridor traffic control (Chapter VI);

6. outlined collaborative experiments (see in particular Annex 1) using the existing traffic corridor facilities (especially in the fields of automatic incident detection and driver response to variable directional information) and initiated a number of small national pilot studies with the aim of developing ideas and concepts which have arisen directly from the Group's discussions.

I.4 Significance of the ICE-Project

The importance of traffic corridor control lies in the breadth of impact that improved systems yield. Traffic corridor control is related to optimum road maintenance schemes, improved utilisation of space devoted to road traffic, and to priority bus lane systems; it also responds to safety, environmental and energy requirements.

The significance of the ICE-Project should be measured not only in terms of the results of the co-operative projects, but in terms of having established a new tool for international co-operative road transport research. This new tool consists of sharing not only research results, but actually undertaking research on a joint international basis. Considering the complexity of the task of actually "doing" research together - namely, several OECD participants from countries of Europe, Japan or the United States - and of planning, executing, evaluating and distributing results, the accomplishments to date, during the three-year time frame of the Group, have been most gratifying. The Group has learned much, but also leaves many unanswered questions. The key to success is, of cource, the technical excellence of the research being performed. In addition, proper organisation and management of such an effort is most important. It is in these later phases where the Group has also made some progress. The framework developed will not only exist for performing international corridor experiments, but can be applied also to other appropriate road research areas.

II

OBJECTIVES AND CRITERIA OF TRAFFIC CORRIDOR CONTROL

The basic aim of traffic corridor control is to improve overall cost effectiveness through optimising the utilisation of the road network within the corridor. The overall community costs with respect to road traffic comprise two categories of cost items: (1) the direct costs to the road user, both local and through traffic; and (2) the indirect costs to the residents within or adjacent to the corridor. Accidents, journey times, fuel consumption, unexpected delay, irritation and discomfort of drivers are examples of the former category; air pollution, noise, vibration and some of the effects of accidents are examples of the latter.

Minimisation of overall journey time is a widely accepted direct aim in most cases because its economic benefit is relatively large and measurable; furthermore it is of prime importance to the driving public. However, minimisation of overall journey time does not always accord with minimisation of individual journey times, especially under regularly or predictably loaded conditions. Therefore consideration should be given to individuals as far as possible but consistent with community benefit in order to maintain motorists' reliance on the system.

Improving safety is considered to be an essential criterion in every circumstance. Measures to enhance safety in the case of hazardous conditions are particularly important although the measurable economic benefits might not be as large as those arising from efficient emergency and post crash traffic control.

Maximising throughput of traffic for the whole corridor in terms of either number of vehicles or number of persons is one of the main aims, particularly in cases of blockage, oversaturation and the immediate aftermath of major incidents. This coincides with minimising overall journey time as well as minimising unexpected delay in such circumstances and also helps to decrease several other cost items mentioned above.

Maintaining uniform traffic speed through the reduction and elimination of undue speed change and stop-and-go operations can be a desirable aim for many reasons, particularly relative to safety, energy consumption, the environment and individual driving comfort.

To ensure safe and efficient guidance of drivers through the corridor is also a commonly accepted aim of corridor control. This, however, is considered to be rather a comprehensive expression of control means for realising various objectives than a criterion itself.

It has been pointed out that since accident rates are usually different between motorways and other roads there may possibly be a trade off between improving safety and saving journey time in traffic diversion control. Increased environmental hazards caused by traffic diverted to alternative routes may also be subject to a similar trade off.

It has been recognised by the Group that criteria for corridor control may differ depending on traffic conditions and control policy and that the choice regarding the priority of objectives should be made for each system by individual countries considering the local conditions. The criterion may change for a single system depending on the prevailing traffic situation; e.g. minimising overall journey time under predictably loaded conditions and improving safety and maximising throughput under unpredictable hazardous conditions.

The means for realising these objectives, which at the same time constitute the goals of corridor control as well, include the following:

i) increase efficiency of traffic diversion (Section III.2.2), ramp control (Section III.2.3), linear (lane and speed) control (Section III.2.4), emergency traffic control and other traffic condition dependent control means;

ii) provide rapid detection and advanced warning of disturbances, timely assistance to stranded motorists, and removal of capacity-reducing incidents especially for decreasing unexpected delay (Section III.3); and,

iii) provide good communication to drivers in order to inform them regarding traffic and road conditions ahead and appropriate actions they should take (Section III.4).

It is recognised that the above classification of major goals of corridor control is somewhat arbitrary due to the interrelated nature of these goals and the corresponding remedial traffic control measures to be applied.

It is essential that drivers be convinced of the effectiveness and reliability of such a system and the advantages offered (see Section III.5). Short-term prediction of traffic conditions together with automatic incident detection and efficient communications is considered to be a major problem to be solved in order to assure drivers' reliance on the system.

III

REVIEW OF CONCEPTS

III.1 Systems Description

In this report a corridor is defined as a system of parallel or almost parallel routes which link an origin and a destination area and vice versa; these routes are connected in such a way that drivers may divert to alternative routes if they know or are convinced that the route which they take presents less traffic difficulty at a certain moment than other routes or route sections of the corridor.

Corridor control is aimed at guiding drivers to their destinations in the case of unexpected difficulties in a section of the corridor through the use of a more advantageous route and at avoiding traffic congestion and stops. This applies, for instance, in the following cases:

i) the capacity of a corridor section can temporarily not satisfy an exceptionally high traffic demand;

ii) the capacity of a corridor section is temporarily reduced due to hazardous conditions, incidents, etc., although traffic demand is not unusually increased.

The limits of a corridor control scheme are reached when the total capacity of all routes is less than total demand. This is especially the case if capacities are temporarily reduced due to accidents. Therefore, the diversion and route guidance system of the corridor is often supplemented by control schemes that aim at accident prevention by:

- advanced hazard warning;
- traffic actuated variable speed limit signs designed to provide a minimization of speed differences (and to ensure maximum throughput), and
- lane control to avoid the build-up of queues, and guide drivers from obstructed lanes to other lanes on the same carriageway.

The principle of a two-route corridor system is shown in Figure III.1 (one direction only; see also Annex 2), as well as the essential corridor control systems:

- diversion of traffic before entering the corridor (advisory or mandatory);

- diversion of traffic using the corridor (advisory or mandatory);

- protection against oversaturation on motorways by means of ramp metering or ramp closure;

- prevention of accidents by means of warning systems, speed control and lane control.

In this figure the width of the road corresponds to its capacity. The arrows superimposed on the roadway represent, by their shaft width, existing volume or, if accompanied by a D, the traffic demand of the upstream route section. If the arrow shaft width is equal to the roadway width, then capacity is fully utilized. If it is larger (see extreme left-hand side of figure) it is necessary to "deviate" part of the traffic demand.

The dashed arrows show the directions in which traffic has to be guided by means of the corridor control system. Careful examination of this figure reveals the large amount of data needed to be collected and analysed continuously in order to ensure a highly reliable control system.

The symbols of the traffic signs depicted in Figure III.1 are only indicative of the sign face to be activated. The symbols do not show the techniques used for variable signing. Red cross and green arrow symbols (in the upper right of the figure) have been used to represent lane control measures but other symbols are also possible. In the lower right side of the figure is presented a traffic detour priority sign, which can be important as a control measure at exit ramps or for guiding traffic back to the motor-way. This type of priority traffic should be allowed more green time at the entry points to the normal urban area traffic control system. This technique has been used in some cases to give priority to buses or other vehicles in the corridor or parts of it.

It is apparent from Figure III.1 that for corridor control systems, the following facilities are needed:

- a detection system which provides the actual data and allows certain predictions to be made;

- a control centre which transforms the detector information into control measures;

- a communication system which presents the decisions of the control centre to the driver, and

- a transmission system of the data from the detectors to the centre and from the centre to the driver and back.

These sub-systems, together with the expected reaction of the driver observed by the detection system, are schematically presented in Figure III.2.

This figure also shows the minimum equipment needed for these sub-systems. Even in the case of minimum facilities, a control system which guides the deviated drivers to their destinations is indispensible; as a rule, this system will be composed of remote-controlled variable direction signs located at the roadside. With most corridor control systems, the essential cost factor concerns the transmission system, for which, up to now, cables and multiplexing equipment have been preferred. There is a need for cheap and mobile corridor control systems which could be temporarily used at bottlenecks to account for increasing traffic until more roads or roads with more capacity are available (for example, the N1 Corridor, Switzerland).

The basic premise for any highly effective corridor control system is an efficient on-line control strategy.

Figure III.1

SCHEMATIC OF CORRIDOR CONTROLS
(one direction only)

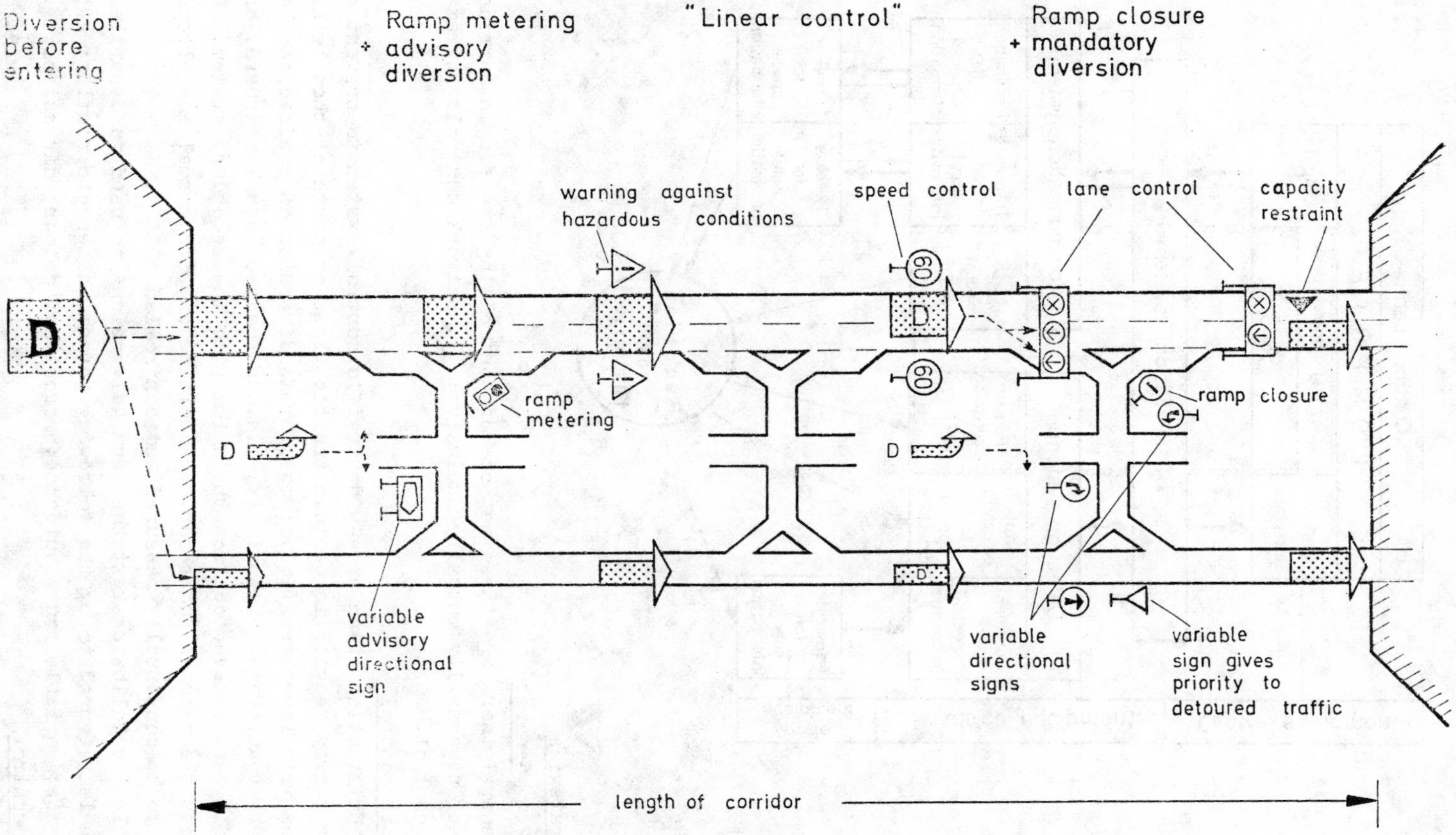

capacity restraint

ramp closure

variable sign gives priority to detoured traffic

lane control

variable directional signs

speed control

Ramp closure
+ mandatory diversion

warning against hazardous conditions

"Linear control"

ramp metering

variable advisory directional sign

Ramp metering
+ advisory diversion

length of corridor

Diversion before entering

15

Figure III.2
SYSTEM EQUIPMENT AND FUNCTION FOR CORRIDOR CONTROL

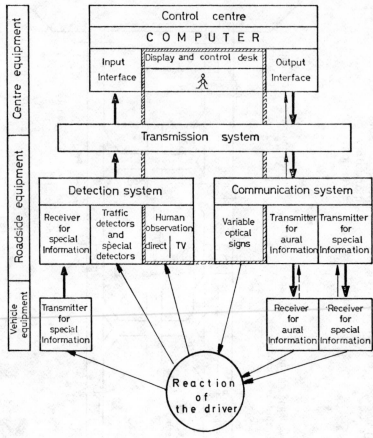

III.2 Strategies

III.2.1 General

In general there are three methods of controlling traffic in corridors although they are not necessarily mutually exclusive: 1. network control; 2. ramp control; 3. linear control.

Network control

Utilisation of an area-wide traffic control system to prevent overloading of the motorway results in certain traffic flows or parts of them being diverted to routes with lower traffic volumes. This diversion of traffic can be made using the primary road system exclusively, i.e. on roads of equal standard, or, alternatively, traffic can be diverted from the primary to the secondary system. During this process the volumes and reserve capacities of both normal and alternative routes have to be continually measured and controlled.

In the following text the term "diversion" is used to describe the operation which is referred to by the following terms: alternate routing; alternate route guidance; variable route guidance; rerouting; detour; diversion.

Ramp control

Ramp control systems are basically aimed at reduction of traffic congestion and improvement of traffic flow on a motorway (or in a corridor) by limiting the number of vehicles which can enter from the ramps as a function of the volume and density of traffic on the motorway. Ramp control systems require that traffic flow measurements be made primarily on the motorway under observation, and/or the routes forming the corridor as well as, normally, the ramps. Although the occurence of traffic congestion can be minimised by means of ramp control, as distinct from network control, diverted traffic is not regulated.

Linear control

Linear control, involving the use of variable message signs and, possibly, other devices, is aimed at providing control of lane usage and traffic speeds in order to optimise corridor throughput and safety. Speed control, with the objective of maintaining optimum vehicular speeds for the prevailing traffic conditions, lane control, with the objective of optimising the distribution of traffic on the existing motorway lanes, and merging control, with the objective of maintaining favourable traffic conditions at merge locations, can all be considered within linear control systems.

The question of whether traffic is controlled before or after entering the corridor is a matter of defining the corridor limits. This determination does not influence the control strategy as such.

III.2.2 Network control - diversion

System and Traffic Structure

If traffic is to be controlled on one or more route segments, it is first necessary to examine the diversion possibilities. In most cases these possibilities depend on the system structure and can be determined by a combination of analysis of the local traffic and roadway characteristics, interviews, and test journeys.

The most desirable alternative routes are those which are of the same length or only slightly longer than the normal route and which do not increase the travel time considerably. The control method for this case of a "parallel corridor" is simple. However, in the case of larger factors of diversion (i.e. length of alternative route divided by length of normal route), the method to be chosen must be based on more precise traffic structure data to ensure effective traffic control (Figures 1 and 2 of Annex 3).

The capacity of the normal and alternative routes has to be examined. This can be done either analytically, i.e. by calculation, or by empirically measuring the fundamental relations between traffic volume, density and speed at different points; more precise information is generally obtained by careful measurements.

Besides data on service volume, the following traffic flow data are required:
- the ratio of through traffic to total traffic; and,
- average travel speed or average travel time.

Through traffic data are measured between corridor entry and exit and registered as parameters in an origin-destination matrix (O-D matrix). There can be different O-D matrices for different cases (Figure 3 of Annex 3). Travel time and travel speed are then determined for the O-D volumes (Figure 4 of Annex 3).

These various traffic parameters are the basis for most control models. However the precision of the data and its usage during control differ in each control model.

Control and Performance Parameters

The operational objective of a control procedure consists of minimising average or total travel time, total delay in certain critical route sections, queues, or the number of vehicles approaching a congested section.

The procedure adopted also aims at minimising, at least in part, the differences in average travel speed either on successive route sections or in successive time intervals.

Furthermore average total travel speeds can be maximised within the boundaries of speed limits relative to volume changes.

As a result the parameters ("target quantities") that are generally considered when optimising control are:
- travel time;
- travel speed;
- delay; and,
- queues.

It should be pointed out that it may be possible to use criteria such as noise, air pollution, energy and safety indirectly through the parameters mentioned above. However, in other circumstances, more direct measurements may be required.

Two parameters are generally used for the performance evaluation of control actions:
- travel time;
- travel speed.

These quantities can be determined by observing vehicle platoons, by noting the passage of individual vehicles (e.g. recording of license plate numbers), or by measurements using representative vehicles in random tests. Representative vehicles can be either specially equipped measuring cars or simply taxis that travel from an origin located before the corridor to a destination beyond it. Travel time and travel speed can also be determined using traffic counts and density measurements.

Another criterion for evaluating the performance of control actions is the "queue". Measuring queues, however, is very complicated (e.g. from a helicopter) as the position of the congestion in time and space generally cannot be predicted. Moreover, a queue is not clearly definable if it results from the capacity of the road being exceeded. Difficulty is also encountered in the interpretation of a queue in before/after studies.

Control Models

Control models are used to obtain the most effective control action by optimising the "target quantities". The models can be very simple or may be based on very complicated mathematical algorithms.

The following are examples of control models:
1. Comparison of measured traffic volumes with established threshold values using a logic of decisions and choice of the most appropriate control plan from a set of previously determined schemes.

   This "logic of decision" system includes every control point on the normal route and the alternative routes. Measurements are carried out of such parameters as volume, density, speed and queue length and comparisons are made with the appropriate threshold values, showing if and how many vehicles have to be diverted in order to keep traffic flowing. The threshold values are determined so as to prevent unstable flow conditions if the values are slightly exceeded. For example the threshold values for volume might be 80 per cent of the maximum admissible traffic volume. In the case of large volume increases, these volumes must be reduced and an O-D matrix is used as a means of determination with regard to the amount of traffic to be diverted from individual route sections. The effectiveness of such control can be improved by basing the control decisions on the comparison of on-line and historical traffic data and on short-term predictions.
2. Analysis of traffic flow of all routes or the critical route sections in regular intervals of one to five minutes.

   In some control models the basis of calculation is the critical queue, in others the density wave or shock wave.

The critical queue results from the saturation flow at the "bottleneck" and from the acceptable travel time difference between the normal and the alternative route (Annex 4). The speed of the contra flow moving density wave is obtained in the manner described in Annex 3. In both cases the number of vehicles driving into the congested area is optimised.

More mathematically oriented control models are based on linear programming (Annex 5). If the potential of these models is to be fully exploited the additional on-line measurements of traffic data are very important.

Short-term Prediction

In complex traffic situations it may not be sufficient to give drivers advanced warning based on traffic conditions at the exact time of the message. The message itself will change the situation, so that when drivers actually reach the trouble-spot, they may encounter quite different conditions from those previously displayed. The message may then seem to have been misleading, perhaps under some circumstances causing distrust of the system. In extreme cases control instability will arise with congestion occuring first at one point on the network then at another. In such complex situations, it is clearly desirable that control decisions leading to the display of messages should embody an allowance for the effect they are likely to cause. Thus it is desirable to have a prediction of the network traffic pattern in the immediate future available at the control centre.

In France a theoretical approach is being developed which depends on the progressive updating of the elements of the O-D matrices for the network. In its simplest form the method assumes that no point in the network is loaded to capacity; it is being extended to include congested conditions. The method has not yet been given a practical test.

An experimental short-term prediction system will be provided as part of the new control system for the Tokyo Expressway. It incorporates a simplified simulation of the traffic flow based on assumed flow-density relationships, for each section of the network. When a blockage occurs on the Expressway, control personnel will be able to compare the results of several alternative closure plans almost simultaneously.

Short-term prediction techniques are at an early stage in their development. It appears likely that they will become more and more necessary as corridor complexity increases. Research on this topic should be encouraged.

Simulation Studies

Traffic simulation by computer is often used in preparatory studies before final decisions on diversion facilities for traffic corridors are taken. Computer programs for off-line simulation are constructed in a way that permits simulation of traffic flow in the part of the network in question. There are two different types of research to be carried out:

1. Development of theoretical traffic relationships

   In this type of simulation model, a range of input traffic volumes are systematically related to all factors that have an effect on traffic flow. Results will be in the form of calculated parameters or distribution functions by means of which it will be possible to quantify possible influences on traffic flow. These parameters and functions will then be used as a basis for the control strategies and models. A considerable control model simplification will be achieved by this method, provided that parameters and functions can be automatically monitored and continuously adapted to altering conditions.

2. Evaluation of operational strategies

In this case different traffic volumes, either measured in the corridor or estimated, will be preset for off-line simulation. This simulation serves for the determination of optimal diversion plans, or already existing plans will be played through and checked with regard to their application possibilities. The special advantage of simulation is that not only diversion plans but also control models as such can be evaluated and verified. Before the first application of the strategy, possible effects will be estimated by simulation. During activity, control measures will be stored on-line, together with traffic characteristics. Subsequently they will be simulated and evaluated.

Thus, simulation is able to fulfil mainly the following tasks:
- investigations of the effects of various parameters;
- calculation of suitable diversion plans;
- analysis of manually calculated diversion plans;
- global examination of projected control models.

Furthermore, on-line simulations can also be constructed as control models. This method, however, demands a considerable amount of computer time and storage capacity.

III.2.3 Ramp control

Aims of Ramp Control

The basic aims of motorway entrance ramp control may be one or all of the following:
1. Reduction of traffic congestion and improvement of traffic flow on the motorway.
2. Increase in traffic flow on heavily trafficked sections.
3. Reduction of overall travel time.
4. The possibility of balancing traffic flow between the motorway and alternative routes.
5. Installation of a system ensuring for the users problem-free travel on the freeway allowing them choice of route according to waiting time.
6. Reduction of conflicts and, consequently, of accidents occurring at merging points.
7. Maintenance of stable freeway traffic conditions, meterable and controllable in accordance with freeway capacity.

While the joint pursuance of these several aims is, admittedly, feasible, it should be borne in mind that aims 4 and 5 must be considered in the context of traffic control in a corridor with alternative routes.

As to goal 6, this entails, as will be described later, the availability and implementation of equipment and strategies of greater complexity than for the other aims.

Ramp Control Strategies

The implementation of a ramp control system always entails the installation of traffic signals. The operation of the traffic signals provides the means of controlling with precision ramp traffic flow according to the selected criteria. Several strategies, ranging from the simple to the sophisticated can be applied:

1. Periodical closure

In certain specific cases, ramp control will consist only in systematically closing the ramp during certain peak-traffic periods. These periods will be selected on the basis of statistical data concerning traffic conditions. However, the system, which requires minimal equipment, presents the drawback of not allowing for the real capacity of the motorway at the time of closure and of enforcing an authoritative measure which is not necessarily justified. The system may nevertheless prove

adequate for the control of well-established recurrent conditions such as peak
weekend traffic.

2. <u>Fixed-time metering</u>

All control strategies, other than ramp closure as described above, aim at controlling ramp flow, i.e. by controlling the number of vehicles or by setting the
release rate.

The simplest form of metering is, naturally, by means of a traffic light operating
on a fixed-cycle basis. The parameters of the cycle (proportion and duration of
green light) are determined according to traffic characteristics measured before
the system is commissioned. Several programmes can be used and subsequently
selected by period of day. The operation then proceeds in the same manner as that
of most traffic signals controlling urban intersections. However, like ramp
closure, the system suffers from the drawback of not allowing for traffic flow
variations which often obtain on motorways, and of severe disruptions as may be
caused by traffic incidents or accidents.

3. <u>"Demand-capacity" control</u>

With this system, the operating cycle of ramp signals varies in response to the
real characteristics of the traffic. The cycle is determined by measuring the
downstream capacity and the upstream demand of the motorway. The release rate is
such that the capacity of the motorway is never exceeded by the released ramp
volume.

Measurement of the capacity is effected by measuring the traffic volume on the
motorway and by comparing this with the result of previous experience showing the
real capacity of the motorway. It should however be pointed out that the measurement of traffic flow is not a sufficient criterion because, though a low figure may
indicate ample capacity margin, it could well be symptomatic of incipient congestion. This calls for the measurement of an additional parameter such as speed.
Tentatively, the system can be operated on the basis of volume and capacity measurements in the shoulder lane only, thereby minimising variations due to merging
vehicles. However, this system will not optimise motorway flow.

4. <u>Occupancy control</u>

Release rate parameters are determined on the basis of occupancy measured upstream
of the ramp. The occupancy rate is the percentage during which a given point of the
roadway is occupied by vehicles and is therefore highly indicative of traffic
conditions. For example, an occupancy rate of less than 15 per cent corresponds to
smooth traffic flow. Used jointly with measurement of speed, this parameter will
also provide a measure of flow rates.

In the case of responsive ramp control, occupancy is generally measured upstream of
the ramp. Release rates are based on statistical data bringing into play pre-set
thresholds and knowledge of the downstream capacity of the motorway.

5. <u>Gap acceptance control</u>

The above-described responsive-control strategies are based on the overall condition
of motorway traffic and on the measurement of general parameters. In the case of
gap acceptance control, the strategy takes a discrete form, based on individual
vehicles. Control is then based on the detection, on the ramp-side lane, of gaps
of acceptable length so that the vehicles released from the ramp may merge into the
motorway traffic without disrupting traffic flow.

Several methods may be used. The simplest form consists in detecting, by means of
two detectors located on the shoulder lane, gaps which exceed the control parameter

(critical gap) established by traffic conditions on the motorway. In order to allow for vehicle motion, speed measurements must also be carried out so as to match the travel time of the ramp vehicle from its start at the ramp signal with the travel time of the acceptable gap to the merge area.

6. Moving-merging control

This control system is a refinement of the previous method. The system provides the driver with a continuous display as he moves down the ramp, towards the merging area. Acceptable gaps are determined on the shoulder lane and a series of "pacer" lights mounted a few metres apart light up in sequence so as to control the speed of the vehicle and guide the driver to the detected gap.

The system is particularly effective where sub-standard geometrics make the merging operation particularly hazardous, for example where there are inadequate acceleration lanes, as often happens on old motorways.

7. Gap-acceptance/demand-capacity combination

The demand-capacity method would provide for macroscopic control, whereas the gap-acceptance system would allow microscopic control. The "combination" of the two systems enables merge-rate determination according to the demand-capacity principle and vehicle merging on the gap acceptance principle.

8. Integrated system operation

The different systems described above consider the ramp as an independent system, allowing only for traffic immediately upstream and downstream of the ramp. In most urban corridors, ramps are sited successively over relatively short distances and in many cases consideration must be given to the whole system.

The simplest form of integrated system operation is a fixed-time one where metering rates are calculated from historical data to give an optimum solution for the whole system.

Integrated traffic-responsive metering is a complex operation requiring sophisticated strategies and central computer control in order to calculate ramp control parameters in accordance with traffic conditions along the whole length of the motorway. This calls for the use of strategies which outrange the scope of ramp control proper and should be considered within the overall context of corridor control.

Ramp Control Efficiency

At the time of preparing this report, few countries had installed complete ramp control systems, except in the United States, where although limited in numbers, efficiency measurements were made.

Control performance. Rather than attempting to establish overall performance criteria, a difficult task due to the lack of statistical significance, a few typical experimental results from the United States can be quoted:

- Los Angeles - Harbour Freeway

  Control of six ramps with predetermined phasing and periodical closure. A 100 per cent increase in speed has been noted (35 to 70 km/h) and cumulative time savings of some 1,000 hours per day.

- Los Angeles - Chula Vista Project

  Four controlled ramps. Traffic speed on the freeway has increased by 65 per cent.

- Chicago - Dan Ryan Expressway

  Control of four ramps by a one-at-a-time system which is manually controlled. Average time saving of five minutes over a section of six kilometres. Five per cent increase of traffic volume during peak hour.

- Chicago - Eisenhower Expressway

  Control of four ramps by a one-at-a-time system with release rates variable from five to fifteen seconds during peak hours, (waiting times at signals included). Substantial decrease in numbers of accidents and periods of traffic congestion.
- Houston - Gulf Freeway

  Approximately 55 per cent increase of traffic speed on the freeway, ten per cent increase of traffic volume during peak hours and 30 per cent decrease in accident rate.
- Dallas - North Central Expressway

  Control of 35 ramps. Fifteen per cent increase of speed on the freeway and 45 per cent decrease in accident rate.

An interesting example in Europe is to be found in Italy; however, operational results are not yet available as the traffic volumes are low because the tollway is not yet completed:

- Naples, Italy. East-West Tollway

  Control of 18 ramps by central digital computer with local analogue computer stand-by. Six classes of "admittance", with choice of class dependent on main flow traffic density. Each class of admittance is defined by a given ratio of ramp green to red times: actual timing determined by real time detected demand of ramp traffic; in case of queue on ramp, automatic switching to next higher admittance class.

Traffic control by systematic ramp closure is used in Japan and constitutes in the case of the Tokyo Expressway the major and the only direct tool for controlling demand. The main features of the system used and its performance are as follows:

- Tokyo Expressway

  Every half an hour during the day time hours, several on-ramps are selected to be closed for the next half an hour. The control policy is such that no ramp is kept closed for more than half an hour except in the case of serious incidents on the expressway. The radio broadcast stations frequently tell drivers the locations of the ramps to be closed in the next half an hour.

  This on-off control of ramps has an advantage in that waiting queues of vehicles on the ramps which are quite probable to occur when ramp metering is applied can be avoided. On urban motorways where the ramps are usually short, long waiting queues on the ramps often tend to disturb surface street traffic. The half-hour period was chosen mainly based on the consideration of this queue problem. The experience on the Tokyo motorway indicates that very few drivers wait at the closed ramps. A shorter period, however, might induce more drivers to wait for reopening of the ramps. No method for solving the theoretically optimum set of ramps to be closed in each half-hour period has yet been obtained.

The main conclusions which can be drawn from these examples are that ramp control and closure generally result in a decrease of overall travel times (including waiting times at the ramp for traffic using the motorway), a substantial increase in average freeway speed and a decrease of traffic congestion periods as well as in the numbers of accidents.

Comparative efficiency of different strategies. To validate selection between the various types of control systems proposed and described in the previous sections, a comparative evaluation of the performance of the various strategies would be useful. Unfortunately, significant comparative results are not currently available. However, a number of selection criteria can be established on the basis of the characteristics of the various strategies.

- In the case of well-designed ramps, in particular of modern motorways with long enough acceleration lanes, traffic responsive control systems based on gap acceptance are not necessary and a demand-capacity or occupancy control system is much more advantageous.
- Occupancy control as part of a demand-capacity strategy has proved highly efficient.
- Gap acceptance control may be advantageous on older motorways where merging takes place in poor conditions due to limited visibility, ill-adapted acceleration lanes, gradients, etc.
- Moving merging control systems appear to give good results, facilitating, among other advantages, merging in difficult cases.
- One-at-a-time signal operation limits ramp capacity to approximately 800 vehicles per hour due to the time required for operation of the signal phases.
- Signal performance proper: a French experiment conducted on a ramp serving the A6 motorway has yielded some valuable results. Several control systems were tested:
    - one-at-a-time system release with fixed cycles;
    - platoon-release, with fixed cycles;
    - traffic responsive control.

The one-at-a-time system yielded good merge performance, but, motorists being unaccustomed to this type of control (to date, no such system has been operated on French roads), two-at-a-time release was frequently observed. Platoon-release was more easily understood, being more in keeping with customary practice - though it was found occasionally to create awkward merge situations.

III.2.4 Linear (speed and lane) control

As pointed out in Section III.2.1, "linear" traffic control techniques include primarily measures aimed at optimum lane usage and the utilisation of variable speed limits. Ramp merging to increase throughput and safety can be considered as forming part of ramp control (see also Section III.2.3).

Aims of Linear Control

The basic principle of linear control is to provide special traffic signals along the carriageway (or along individual lanes), thereby enabling variable control according to prevailing traffic conditions.

The prime purpose of this type of control (as against ramp control) is to maintain a satisfactory level of service, in keeping with existing traffic volumes, allowing for sudden changes in freeway capacity caused by the occurrence of unexpected incidents, accidents, roadworks, etc.

Within the context of an overall corridor control system, ramp control, in principle, ensures traffic volumes compatible with disturbance-free traffic flows. However, the need may exist for the installation of a lane and speed control system to control traffic flow disturbed by an incident (see Section III.3) or altered by certain vehicle movements. In certain specific cases imposed by existing design features, special points such as narrowing-down (e.g. lane drops) or merging zones may necessitate special control in order to minimise conflicts between various vehicular streams.

Three different objectives for linear control, each entirely independent of the others and yet applicable individually or jointly, exist. Differences relate primarily to the characteristics of the type of signing to be installed.

The three main objectives are:

1. Speed control
   The various aspects of this objective are to ensure stable flow conditions, to optimise traffic flow by maintaining the "ideal" speed and finally to enhance traffic safety, to reduce the acceleration noise, and thereby, petrol consumption.

2. Lane control
   Urban motorways are affected by frequent traffic incidents which may modify freeway capacity. Detection of these disturbances and the installation of facilities enabling traffic diversion result in significant gains in traffic safety and flow conditions (see also Section III.3, Incident Problem).

3. Merging control (other than ramp merging)
   Disturbances can occur more or less permanently when several vehicular streams are merging or at weaving sections. This is the case with narrowing sections and with weaving sections of two motorways or at certain interchanges. Control at this level makes it possible to "adapt" existing design standards to prevailing traffic conditions.

   The installation of control equipment for one or several of the above-mentioned objectives also makes it possible to achieve secondary objectives which, although they do not by themselves warrant such installation, are nevertheless quite important. The following secondary objectives can be mentioned:

4. Capacity limitation
   In certain cases, for example when the freeway terminates against a "wall" formed by a saturated urban network, there might be an advantage in closing one or several freeway lanes so as to allow traffic only on those lanes which will easily negotiate the "wall".

5. Lane reservation
   Closure of one or several lanes for special purposes.

6. Use of the carriageway in two directions
   Closure of one or several lanes in the normal direction of traffic and allocating them to traffic in the other direction.

7. Miscellaneous information
   The installation of variable message signs may enable the display of valuable information, independent of normal control information (ice and fog conditions, roadworks, etc.).

Speed Control

Experience shows that the dense traffic flow on a motorway in the stage which precedes saturation has an unstable character. Each driver knows only the local characteristics of traffic flow and adapts his speed to them. This unstability can be explained by cybernetics. There is a simple relation between the movements of a vehicle and that of the preceding vehicle. In a queue of vehicles, there is no direct relation between the first vehicle and the last one and the system operates in an open loop. The differential equation which relates the movements of the vehicles which follow each other contains an effect of delay due to the driver's reaction time, a delay which accumulates along the platoon of vehicles. It has been proved that such a system is of necessity unstable. In order to make it stable drivers require information in addition to the knowledge of the behaviour of the vehicle directly in front of him.

The foregoing illustrates the advantages of a road user information system indicating the desirable speed that drivers should keep to.

Strategy to control traffic. For each given volume (or density) there is a certain maximum speed corresponding to stable flow conditions. In addition, this type of control makes it possible to slow down the vehicles upstream of the point where traffic is disturbed or stopped.

The choice of the speeds to be displayed can be effected in two different manners:
- determination of an optimum speed according to the traffic volume on individual roadway sections;
- comparison of traffic characteristics existing over two successive sections and choice of a speed, for the first section, allowing relatively smooth transitions into the next section.

Techniques. Many techniques can be employed which can be distinguished by:
- the method of information of the road users:
    Information can concern the whole carriageway of the motorway or each particular lane.
- the types of information used:
    Advisory speeds, upper speed limits, or range of speeds (including an upper speed limit and a lower speed limit).

Information on the (enforced or recommended) speed as well as the selection of these speeds by the help of a control logic must refer to successive roadway sections, so as to form a system sufficiently flexible to allow for local, often unpredictable modifications of traffic conditions.

Parameters. On the basis of these techniques, speed controls may differ depending on the parameters used in the control logic (software). The main parameters are:
- traffic flow characteristics /speed-flow, speed occupancy, average speed (arithmetic or harmonic)7;
- the time basis on which these data are calculated (for example one, two or five minutes or the time necessary to take 10 or twenty vehicles into account);
- the distance between two different information displays with a minimum practical distance of about three to five hundred metres.

Constraints. Independent of the techniques and parameters chosen, a speed control system will not act satisfactorily if the following requirements are not met:
- an acceptable level of driver compliance;
- accurate information on the degree of driver compliance;
- minimisation of the difference between displayed speeds and actual speeds under the prevailing operating conditions.

Lane Control

Lane control strategies are mainly aimed at controlling the effects of incidents or obstructions on traffic flow (see Section III.3 on the incident problem). Irrespective of the origin of the traffic disturbance (accident, roadworks, vehicle breakdown, etc.), the consequences are always the closure of one or several lanes, at a given point. When advance warning of the disturbances is available, which is the case for example with roadworks, the installation of movable signs (panels, cones, etc.) enables traffic to "conform" with minimum disruption to the reduction in capacity resulting from the lesser number of lanes.

According to this objective, the purpose of lane control is to provide a system which will make it possible to absorb, in similar fashion, disturbances caused by unforeseen events (as to time and location) such as accidents or vehicle breakdowns.

The basic principles of the strategy will, accordingly, be the following:
1. Detection of traffic incidents and assessment of their magnitude (see Section III.3);
2. Determination of measures to be taken so that the residual capacity of the motorway be fully utilised and that traffic flow be least perturbed and remain as smooth as possible.

Obviously, the first point poses the most delicate problems because it entails the use of relatively complex logics if this operation is to be fully automated.

Once the disturbance is identified, the gantry signals can be used to inform users that one or several lanes are closed (often in the form of a red cross and a green arrow signal system). The gantries located upstream of the controlled point will display indications that will enable drivers to negotiate the bottleneck without excessive disruption of the traffic flow (speed limitation and lane switching panels).

Merging Control (other than ramp merging)

The signalling system to be installed to indicate lane closure can be used upstream of merge points (several lanes into a single lane). Flow measurements for each of the merging lanes make it possible to know the demand conditions and, on the basis of the resulting lane capacity, to direct drivers to specific lanes so that merging, or possibly weaving, may proceed as smoothly as possible.

Control of narrow sections is effected in the same way as for an unforeseen incident with the emphasis placed on the determination of vehicle speeds that will facilitate re-grouping on the residual lanes.

III.3 Incident Problem

III.3.1 Incident definition

An incident is a situation (1) in which a driver would like more information to improve his trip conditions (to decrease travel time or to increase safety or comfort), (2) in which an involved driver would need some kind of help. However it is recognised that it is difficult to give a precise, complete and wholly acceptable definition of a roadway incident and the definition presented should be considered as being tentative.

In this context, it is clear that the field covered by the traffic incident concept may become broader with increasing driver needs. One can distinguish two types of incidents; the first type, which could be named "traffic incident" has an impact on the traffic conditions (traffic volume density, speed and/or safety) of the general flow. The second type, which could be named "vehicle incident", concerns only the vehicle which needs help, especially from the safety point of view.

When considering traffic incidents the case of periodic congestion due to lack of capacity, which can be remedied with corridor traffic control systems, is generally disregarded. It is, however, recognised that any incident management system including the detection of incidents as defined above could also be used to detect the onset of expected or regular traffic overload and not only to identify unexpected congestion due to "traffic" incident. Nevertheless, in practice the boundary lines to be drawn between incident systems proper and traffic flow control schemes may be difficult to define.

To make the above definition clearer, the most frequent situations which are considered today as traffic incidents are listed below:
- traffic accident;
- disabled or stopped vehicle;
- obstacle on the pavement;
- abnormal pavement conditions;
- effects of adverse meteorological conditions.

The incident management system should cover the problems of prediction, prevention, detection and clearance.

III.3.2 Incident prediction

It would be of great interest to identify the duration and location of high incident occurrence in order to alert drivers and/or the traffic operation agency. Relative to safety, it is possible to distinguish the cases of danger due to adverse meteorological conditions alone, due to traffic conditions, or due to a combination of both sets of conditions. Thus, there are:

i) "strategic" incident prediction - statistical measures of number of incidents or of situations likely to lead to incidents - as a decision-making basis for the installation of an incident detection system;

ii) "operational" incident prediction, such as adverse meteorological conditions (fog, rain, ice, etc.) in order to warn drivers. The problem in this area is to develop sensors with high detection and small false alarm rates and to be able to build a cost-effective surveillance and warning system.

iii) "on-line" prediction of traffic conditions (certain volume, density and speed ranges) showing a high degree of incident (accident) occurrence probability. Detection of traffic flow and speed or density may be used to actuate a warning system designed to act on traffic speed or vehicle headways (see Section III.2.3 and III.2.4).

III.3.3 Incident prevention

There are a number of non-traffic control measures to prevent incidents as defined above. They are general road safety measures and need not be examined in the framework of the present report. However, as regards the avoidance of the secondary effects of incidents and obstructions, reference to the potential of linear control measures (Section III.2.4) and incident management schemes (Section III.3.5) should be made.

III.3.4 Incident detection

When an incident has occurred, it is important that the agency responsible for the motorway traffic management be able to detect it quickly and correctly. Detection covers not only the problem of localising (in space and time) the incident that has occurred, but also the problem of identifying its nature and estimating its magnitude, in order to acquire the necessary data for making the right decision and removing the incident and eliminate its consequences.

It is difficult in some instances to separate detection and remedial methods because they may be associated; some type of detection methods being, at least partly, corrective methods at the same time. Nevertheless, for clarity, we shall examine them separately.

The various methods being used or planned either alone or in combination for detecting and reporting incidents are the following:

- emergency communication systems, for example, telephones;
- inspection patrols;
- inspection and "action" patrols;
- visual observation by planes, helicopters, etc.
- standing visual observation by closed circuit television, etc.
- automatic incident detecting loops or other sensors.

Automatic incident detection methods are mostly in the research stage. In the field of "vehicle incident detection", few projects are known. They usually deal with automatic accident detection, either with a passive radio-alarm (actuated by an impact detector on board the vehicle) or with a vibration-sensitive observation network.

Important work is being done in the field of "traffic incident detection". Since according to its definition, this type of incident has an impact on the traffic conditions, the detection methods are based on the study of changes in traffic characteristics. These changes may be observed either in the time distribution of certain traffic parameters at a given point of the motorway, in the space distribution at a given time, or in combinations based on a process of traffic pattern recognition. Problems in this area are to choose the best traffic parameters to be observed, to select adequate traffic sensors or to develop new ones, to choose correct intervals between sensors and to develop satisfactory software.

Research on traffic incident detection using the process of pattern recognition has been carried out in the United Kingdom and in France. In Italy, the project implemented in the Naples Tollway system uses occupancy and speed as the basic parameters, the latter for low traffic conditions. The distribution of data in space and time is analysed in order to detect both the passage of the "shock wave" resulting from a sudden disturbance of the traffic flow and the establishment of anomalous conditions (accumulation of vehicles) due to the presence of lane obstructions (see Annex 6).

While automatic incident detection will not likely be able to identify correctly the nature of the detected incident (neither to detect every incident) it is noteworthy that reported data indicate a substantial shortening of intervention time due to the rapid detection of incident location. It is also important to reduce false alarms to an acceptable level, whilst ensuring, insofar as possible, that no genuine incidents are overlooked.

There seems, therefore, to be a consensus for the time being to associate for incident detection on urban motorways an emergency telephone system, an automatic traffic incident detection system and a closed-circuit television system. With this combination, the automatic detection system is used to give the alarm and to select the correct TV camera to be used to observe the probable incident. Preliminary results found in the Los Angeles experiment are very encouraging. They show a detection rate of 95 per cent and a false alarm rate of 2 per cent. In the future, CCTV techniques may be used for automatic visual incident detection.

III.3.5 Incident clearance and management

Once an incident has been detected and reported, then the action taken by the agency responsible for traffic management will depend on the seriousness of the incident and on the prevailing circumstances. However, the basic aims of dealing with incidents may be summarised as action to:
- preserve life;
- minimise risk of further hazard;
- regulate and restore traffic flow;
- prevent unauthorised access to the site of the incident, e.g. by sightseers and by unauthorised or unwanted vehicles;
- assist road users;
- safeguard property.

Considerable contingency planning and co-ordination between police and traffic agencies are pre-requisites for speedy achievement of these aims. This will cover not only the organisation (and clear lines of responsibility) necessary to ensure quick availability as needed of ambulances, fire-fighting, breakdown and other specialised equipment, but also the organisation necessary to effect proper control of the incident on site, including the putting down of cones and warning signs, control of traffic, institution of pre-planned diversions and so on, as may be appropriate.(1)

The detailed responsibility for handling an incident will normally rest with the personnel on site who are in the best position to assess the needs of the situation and

---

1) See also the OECD Road Research Report on Traffic Operation at Sites of Temporary Obstruction, Paris, February 1973.

to call for such additional assistance and/or equipment as may be wanted. When it is known, however, from the initial incident report that persons are injured or are trapped, then it will be desirable to call in the ambulance and fire services even before an assessment on site is possible. Similarly, it may be appropriate to set immediately any remotely controlled warning signs or signals so as to minimise risk of further hazard.

When an incident involves serious interference with traffic flow, it is important to make adequate provision for traffic control and to make an early estimate of the expected duration of the obstruction so that decisions can be taken on whether to issue radio broadcast announcements or whether to institute diversions. In practice no difficulties are experienced in giving estimated durations with sufficient accuracy for these purposes - thus it is possible fairly readily to forecast whether a closure will be for more or less than, say, 1 hour, even though at an early stage it may not be possible to say whether a long closure will be for 2 hours or 4 hours.

Partly obstructed carriageways pose a question whether or not to allow traffic to continue running. Practice varies. Thus some authorities will allow traffic to pass by an obstruction on the carriageway by using the hard shoulder if it is clear, whilst other authorities insist on keeping the hard shoulder freely available for emergency vehicles.

On the approach to an incident it is common to keep the hard shoulder free of traffic so that emergency vehicles may obtain access, but mention should be made of an alternative arrangement in Germany where stationary vehicles on motorways are required to move to the outer edges of the running lanes so that a free path is available between lines of stationary traffic for use by emergency vehicles. This arrangement is particularly suited to dual two-lane carriageways, which are normal in Germany, but is not so clearly suited to dual three-lane (or more) carriageways.

Emergency and other vehicles providing assistance will normally approach an incident in the same direction as normal traffic flow. If arrival is from the opposite direction this will generally mean that the emergency vehicles go past the incident to the next suitable turning point (which may be an interchange or a gap in the central reservation) and then turn to approach in the normal way. The alternative of bringing vehicles to the site against the normal traffic flow can involve substantial dangers if any vehicles can get past the site of the incident and for this reason the practice is not favoured by many authorities. Nevertheless in extreme situations, and particularly with blockages on both carriageways it may prove the only practicable solution, and care must be taken to minimise the risks involved.

Protection at the site of an incident, and of the tail of a developing queue, are of particular importance. The former involves laying down cones and traffic signs; the latter may also make use of a police car with flashing light reversing along the hard shoulder and keeping station with the end of the traffic queue. This action is considered of particular importance in reducing risks of follow up accidents. In multiple pile up accidents it is not unknown for follow up incidents to continue for some hours after the initial occurrence.

The effective management of an incident is determined largely by the pre-planning activities which allow the various emergency vehicles and services to be made available with the minimum of delay. Speed is of the essence both to limit the effect of the initial incident and to minimise the risk of further occurrences. Traffic control and diversions play a part but more effective action is possible from limiting the initial incident and its effects than is possible by subsequent re-routing and management of traffic.

Some statistical information on closures of motorways in England is given in Annex 7.

III.4 Equipment

III.4.1 General

Although hardware aspects have been excluded from the work of the Group (see Section I.2), a short review of principal techniques is presented below as a background for future work.

A typical corridor control system will involve the use of the following types of equipment:

- detectors for automatic or manual detection of relevant conditions concerning traffic flow and climate;
- transmission system for transmission of information from detectors to control centre and back to control devices and driver information systems;
- control centre for collection and evaluation of detected information, short-term forecasts of flow conditions and decisions of control measures based on criteria for optimum control;
- communication system - traffic control for realisation of control such as traffic diversion, ramp control, lane closures and variable speed signalling;
- communication system - driver information for supplementary information to displayed mandatory signs and pre-warning of unexpected events.

An example of equipment actually used for a corridor control project (Naples Tollway) is given in Table III.1.

III.4.2 Detectors

Detection of traffic flow parameters such as flow, speed, occupancy or density is performed automatically using detectors located at strategic positions in the corridor.

A large number of detector types based on different technical principals are commercially available. Some of the more widely used types are presented in Table III.2.

Inductive loop detectors are widely used in corridor projects for a number of reasons:

- the sensitive area can be easily controlled by means of loop configuration and tuning;
- loops can be used singly or in combination for sensing presence, queue length, speed and vehicle length;
- the method is reasonably accurate and low-cost.

The inductive loop can be rather costly to install when there is heavy traffic flow or in the case of steel or reinforced concrete structures. In these cases and also where numerous overpasses exist ultrasonic or radar detectors might be preferable.

Detection of traffic incidents has been treated in Section III.3.4 above. In this field there is a need for research to find inexpensive and reliable systems.

Detection of climatic conditions such as fog, wind and ice is mostly done automatically with or without manual interpretation and checking to confirm bad visibility or slippery road. Equipment is available for sufficiently accurate detection of the above-mentioned effects when they occur at the site of measurement. The remaining problem however is to be able to forecast these conditions so that proper measures can be taken and advance warnings displayed.

Detectors for carbon-monoxide (CO) and smoke content are presently used only in long tunnels for ventilation control but may get a wider usage in the future.

III.4.3 Transmission

A number of different techniques for data transmission are available and can be applied for corridor control. It is recommended that any specific roadside equipment

Table III.1

EQUIPMENT USED IN NAPLES TOLLWAY CORRIDOR CONTROL PROJECT

	Equipment	Quantity	Type	Function
Control centre	Map display panel	1	Light indicator (540 3-colour indicators)	Traffic situation display
	Control desk: TV monitors	6		Traffic situation display
	Operation desk	1	Pushbuttons (78)	Manual orders
	Loudspeaker	1		Audial alarms
	Drum memory and computer indication	3	Light indicators	
	Digital indication	10		Vehicle counting
	Teleprinter	1		Communication with computer
	Computer	1	Ferrite cores 12K memory, binary number system	Data processing
	Computer	1	Ferrite core 8K	Telemetry
Transmission	Cable		Multiplex system	
Detectors	Loop detectors	540	Inductive 1.8 x 1.8 m	Presence on tollway
	Loop detectors	76	Inductive 2 x 3.5 m	Presence on ramps and exit/entrance
	Loop detectors	42	Inductive 1.8 x 1.8 m	Speed measurements
Controllers	Ramp controllers	18	Analogue density computer	Traffic density
	Tunnel controllers	4	Analogue density computer	Traffic density
Variable signs and signals	Entrance ramps Condition signs	36	Lighting of fixed symbols	3 symbols
	Congested section signs	21	Rotating prisms	3 symbols for 4 sections
	Variable message tape sign	41	Illuminated scroll	30 symbols
	Exit ramps Condition signs	14	Illuminated scroll	30 symbols (normally 9 combinations)
	Repeater sign for exit ramp condition	14	Rotating prisms	3 symbols for 2 exits

Table III.2

TYPES OF DETECTORS PRACTICABLE FOR SURVEILLANCE AND CONTROL

Detector	Measurement capability					Approximate cost - dollar ($)		Comments
	Passage count	Presence	Speed	Occupancy	Queue length	Detector cost	Total including installation	
Inductive Loop	x	x	x	x	x	300	500	
Ultrasonic a) pulsed	x	x	x	x	x	500	600-1,200	Improved speed measurement
b) continuous wave	x		x			1,000	1,000-1,600	
Radar	x		x			500	600-1,200	
Magnetometer	x	x		x		200	350-500	Poorly defined detection zone
Pneumatic	x		x					For temporary use

Reference: P. Everall, FHWA Urban Freeway Surveillance and Control, Washington DC, 1972.

and codes should be compatible with the standard of CCITT (Commission Consultative Internationale de Telegraphie et de Telephonie).

The transmission system first considered in any corridor project should be direct cables. This may be very costly to arrange along an existing road. Once a cable is laid however it is not difficult to obtain up to 500 individual communication channels through a single cable by the use of multiplexing techniques.

Another possibility is to use rented telephone lines. This method may however give rise to a number of technical and administrative problems. Radio transmission is normally not feasible because of the lack of frequencies, high cost, and possible maintenance difficulties.

III.4.4 Control centre

A corridor control project will require a computer with necessary auxiliary equipment for interface and communication. The type of computer selected naturally depends on the size and complexity of the project, generally a small or medium-scale computer with 16 K-32 K words will be sufficient or an equivalent computer configuration.

For many purposes during tests and operations it is practical to have some kind of display equipment in the centre. Features that can be displayed are:
- traffic conditions on critical parts of the system;
- indications from alarm boxes, detectors, etc. and information derived from this;
- status of signals and roadside displays.

This will generally require monitors for a closed-circuit television system as well as panels with multicolour indicator lights and cathod-ray tube devices.

III.4.5 Communication system - traffic control

The need for control equipment depends upon the types of control used in the project.

Control equipment for <u>diversion</u> involves the use of changeable message signs and may be combined with lane control signalling, (see Section III.4.6 on external visual communication below).

Equipment for <u>ramp control</u> is to some extent dependent upon control strategy but usually requires:

- a detector to register the demand of a vehicle on the ramp;
- warning and regulatory signs to tell the drivers that the ramp is controlled and instruct him what action to take on reaching the signal;
- traffic signals on both sides of the ramp; in some cases combined with an automatic barrier;
- pavement markings to indicate the stop line and to restrict the used width of the ramp so that vehicles will pass over the check-in detector. The stop line must be located far in advance of the merging point to allow vehicles to reach adequate merging speed;
- local controllers for the signals. If the ramp control is carried out from a central computer the local controllers will only perform the actual switching of the signals from one aspect to another. The ramp control can also be carried out locally, in which case the controller, depending upon strategy, can be anything from a fixed-time controller to a mini-computer.

<u>Lane control</u> requires special traffic signals for individual lanes, thereby enabling differential control according to traffic conditions on each lane. Gantries, sited at regular intervals, are usually installed for this purpose to support signs assigned to the different lanes. These signs can consist of:

- lane control signals, often with red cross and green arrow;
- changeable message signs of various types giving instructions, warnings or information designed to ensure clearer appreciation of the situation;
- flashing amber lights designed to draw the attention of drivers to the signs.

Apart from the above mentioned special equipment, lane control naturally also requires detectors, transmission system and a control centre for its operation.

III.4.6 <u>Communication system – driver information</u>

Systems for information to drivers in the "MARK 1" technology are based upon one-way communication of information to the drivers. There are three different modes for this:

a) in-vehicle aural communication;
b) in-vehicle visual communication;
c) external visual communication.

Different methods and equipment for all these modes will be tested and the systems compared in large scale in co-operation between a number of European countries (COST 30).

<u>In-vehicle aural communication</u> relies on information from an area broadcasting system and/or local roadside transmission. The roadside transmission can be performed via long inductive loops embedded in the pavement or point-antennas at the side of the road.

<u>In-vehicle visual communication</u>. This method may utilise a display panel in each vehicle with a standardised set of messages which could be illuminated in appropriate combinations to give a range of messages. It could be activated by a digital pulse code transmitted from a small inductive loop in the roadway or a pole mounted aerially. Current research underway in Japan makes use of liquid crystal technology for the in-vehicle display system.

External visual communication of information to drivers, apart from the fixed signs standardized according to the Vienna Convention, is given through changeable message signs. These can be of electro-mechanical or electric type:

Electro-mechanical
. Rotatable laminae
. Prisms
. Scroll
. Continuous strips
. Rollers
. Rollers on continuous belt
. Sliding panel

Electric
. Light matrix

A further description of these techniques is given in Annex 8.

Whereas most fixed signals are visible by means of reflected light many of the variable signs operate by means of transmission of light which makes them visible at a longer distance. However, this may necessitate a revision of the 1968 Vienna Convention, especially to allow the use of light matrices, in view of the problems concerning shape, colour, the definition and the use of light symbols on dark background.

III.5 Driver Response

The effectiveness of corridor control measures depends on the extent to which the information transmitted to drivers is accepted by them. Information can only be accepted if drivers understand it and are ready to act accordingly.

III.5.1 Communication to drivers

Understanding requires that the information be conspicuous, i.e. symbols or signs stand out boldly against the background. Signs which are in accordance with the Vienna Convention usually meet these requirements. The standardized symbols and signs are familiar to drivers throughout the world and there is reasonable hope, that matrix signs will, before long, meet the same requirement.

Spoken and acoustic information not only involves problems of transmission but also those of hearing and language, as well as those of quickness of transmission. For the time being it cannot be taken for granted that spoken and acoustic information will be understood by all drivers on international routes. Whether or not it will be possible to work with internationally agreed acoustic information is still an open question. Information that can be transmitted simultaneously by optical and acoustic means may be particularly promising. However, confronting drivers simultaneously with acoustic and optical informations of different contents should be avoided.

III.5.2 Observance by drivers

In the observance of information drivers may be motivated by the following reasons:
a) A driver knows that it will be in his personal interest to observe the information (gaining time, reduced accident risk, driving ease);
b) A driver has become convinced that it will be in the interest of all drivers - even if in a particular case it is not in his interest, but neither to his disadvantage - if information is observed by him;
c) Non-observance is subject to penalty;
d) Drivers have no alternative, all other routes are closed.

Most control strategies are based on the assumption that drivers will behave as described under (b). If there is a possibility for an individual to decide differently, and if his co-operative spirit is less than it should be, it has to be taken into account that information will be observed by only a part of the driving population, particularly in view of the fact that the information does not in all cases require mandatory action and that non-observance is difficult to prove. Enforcement according to (c) is basically only possible in cases of temporary, complete closures of certain routes, carriageways or lanes. In such cases it may be more effective to work with remote-controlled closure equipment (d).

The most important aim of most corridor control measures, in cases of unexpected peak demands and incidents (accidents), is the diversion of part of the traffic flow for distribution on several alternative routes. It is therefore important to do everything possible to achieve voluntary observance of the given information. That is to say, the control strategy may have to be so designed as to motivate drivers in a positive sense (a), which will possibly compromise the optimum solution.

Detours on routes of inferior quality, poorer throughput conditions (STOP signs, no priority), and poor guide signs result in a low level of compliance. It is essential that control measures not be based on prevailing traffic situations but on the prediction of what will happen. It is essential, as well, that correct predictions be made of the traffic situation on the detour routes drivers are forced to take. In addition, it should be taken into account that drivers will be unfamiliar with detour routes in many cases, so that a factor of uncertainty will also be involved. As a general rule and in the interest of traffic safety, drivers should be informed that they are on a detour route.

III.6 Concluding Remarks

The foregoing discussion of the concepts involved in traffic corridor control has been based on ongoing research and development activities in participating Member countries, most of the results of which have not yet been officially published. This review takes account of theoretical research information on planned and operational corridor facilities (see Annex 2), some experimental work carried out and initial practical experience gained. The research efforts initiated during the Group's work should advance the state-of-the-art in this field, and validate and further develop present traffic corridor control concepts.

IV

ASSESSMENT OF TOTAL SYSTEM

IV.1 Methodology

The assessment procedures presented here(1) include the following:
- Evaluation of the problems
  The system must be designed to aid and service the problems that are experienced
  in each specific corridor.
- Analysis of solutions
  The applicability of the various control strategies described in Sections III.2
  and III.3 together with the equipment implications presented in Section III.4
  must be studied.
- Documentation of results
  It is essential to monitor the operation and efficiency of the system implemented
  in order to determine how well the system objectives are met.

Each aspect of these procedures is discussed in some detail in the following
sections. The economic aspects, that is whether the service provided is worth the costs
involved for installing, maintaining and operating the system, are discussed in
Chaper V.

In assessing the potential application of specific communication or control
strategies, the analyst probably will have to rely on the experience from similar systems which have been installed at other locations such as described in Chapter III and
Annex 2 of this report. But just because some type of control application has been
successfully used in one area, it does not ensure that the same magnitude of improvement can be expected in the corridor being studied in another area. Thus, some
engineering judgment is involved in the corridor assessment procedures.

IV.2 Evaluation of the Problems

The initial step in developing a system to improve traffic operations in any network is to identify the problem areas and to determine the cause, the frequency and the
effects associated with each problem area. Only through the evaluation of quantitative
problem data can effective solutions be found.

In any potential traffic corridor project, there are expected to be three classes
of problems which may be helped from traffic surveillance, communication and control
type of solutions. These three classes of problems consist of:
1. Recurring problems
2. Non-recurring problems
3. Environmental problems

---

1) * Bissell, H., "A Position Paper on the Proposed Integrated Motorist Information
       System Evaluation Program," United States Federal Highway Administration,
       Washington, D.C., 1974.

IV.2.1 Recurring problems

Examples of recurring problems which may be expected to occur in a motorway corridor area are presented in Table IV.1. These problems are arranged into four categories: overloading, merging, turbulence, and exit ramp congestion. Each of these categories is outlined in terms of potential solutions and proposed investigations or studies to evaluate the éxtent each problem exists.

The overloading problem on the motorway facilities is best evaluated through a series of studies to determine the speeds, volumes and densities of the traffic flows throughout the peak traffic periods. These studies can include aerial photography such as has been conducted in a number of urban motorway surveillance and control projects, and/or a series of speed and delay type studies.

Through these studies the bottleneck areas of the motorway facilities are located and more exact capacity quantities and levels of service qualities can be determined. The development of speed-flow-density contour plots, and speed-density profiles are useful tools in determining where the problem areas occur and the extent in both time and distance that the traffic stream is affected.

The alternate routes and surface roadways must also be studied during those peak congested periods to determine when and where significant traffic delays occur on these facilities. Evaluations must be made to determine if there are available reserve

Table IV.1

INVESTIGATION OF SOME RECURRING PROBLEMS

Problems	Potential Solutions	Evaluation Studies Proposed
Overloading	Network control Ramp control	. Analysis of demands and travel times in the corridor . Analysis of traffic patterns through the year . Development of contour plots for speed, flow, density, delay and travel time on the motorway . Determination of total travel and total travel times for the motorway . Analysis of flow-density relationships on the motorway
Merging	Ramp merging control	. Observations of merging operations . Analysis of merge area accident records . Computer simulation of merging control system operation, based on measured ramp and motorway volumes
Turbulence on the motorway	Linear control: . Speed control . Lane control	. Observations . Analysis of moving vehicle data
Exit ramp Congestion	Network control, e.g: . Control of signals adjacent to motorway	. Observations . Review of signal timing . Capacity analysis

capacities on these alternate routes during periods when the recurring congestion occurs on the motorways. Travel time studies on both the motorway and the surface roadways for typical traffic flows are important to the evaluation procedure.

The entrance ramps are points that need special study. It must be determined from visual observation if each ramp is operating satisfactorily or if some remedial treatment is needed to aid the traffic in merging into the motorway stream. In areas where geometrics are restrictive-inadequate acceleration lane, high convergence angle, inadequate sight distance upstream of the ramp nose and/or ramp alignment which does not permit high speed operation - ramp metering and/or merging control facilities may have to be considered.

In addition to the merging problems, ramps must be observed to determine how ramp volumes affect the flow on the main motorway stream of traffic. If heavy ramp traffic demands occur, stop and go operations may prevail on the ramps which will contribute to a high accident rate.

Turbulence may be expected to occur during peak traffic periods when the traffic demand is greatest. When traffic volumes approach the capacity of the motorway, minor fluctuations in traffic speeds are propagated rapidly upstream as "shockwaves". When vehicles enter the disturbance area, their speed is reduced suddenly. These kinematic waves limit the throughput on the motorway and at the same time create a significant safety hazard due to potential rear-end collisions. It is therefore desirable to increase the stability of the traffic and inform approaching motorists of the impending hazard. Traffic stability can be accomplished through speed control.

On many motorway facilities a hazardous situation may occur when exit ramp traffic backs up on the motorway. This may be caused by capacity limitations at the end of the ramp. When an exit ramp has traffic backed onto the motorway, it affects the operation of all motorway lanes.

IV.2.2 Non-recurring problems

Non-recurring problems are associated with capacity reducing incidents on the motorway such as accidents, mechanical breakdowns, roadway maintenance, etc. (see Section III.3). There are several countermeasures which can be employed when such incidents occur which inlcude: detection of incidents, dispatching assistance; warning approaching motorists, diversion of traffic from the motorway, and accommodating diverted traffic on alternate routes. These considerations are summarised in Table IV.2 in terms of the problem, the potential solution, and proposed studies to evaluate the problems.

Studies of the proposed corridor facilities should be conducted to collect incident information to determine the frequency of incident occurrence, their locations, and duration. This can best be done through routine patrol of the facilities and special records kept as to type of incident, time lanes were blocked, estimated duration of the incident and estimated times for detection, for service arrival, and for removal for incidents requiring such service.

Various incident detection and verification systems should be studied to determine the electronic surveillance system requirements to meet the needs of the motorway facilities. An incident detection algorithm will, most likely, influence the configuration and spacing of detectors. Procedures to determine the nature of the incident and the service required, if any, must be developed in order to minimise the adverse effect on traffic movements and to provide optimum service to the vehicle in trouble.

Tableau IV.2

INVESTIGATION OF SYSTEM FUNCTIONS TO COUNTERACT NON-RECURRING PROBLEMS

Functions	Potential Solutions	Evaluation Studies Proposed
Incident detection	. CB Radio . Roadside telephones . Routine motorway patrol . Electronic sensors . Aerial surveillance	. Investigation of patterns of incident occurrence . Investigation of incident detection methodology . Analysis of incident effects on traffic
Dispatching appropriate assistance	. Routine motorway patrol . Long range TV coverage to identify required assistance . Aerial surveillance . Roadside telephones	. Investigation of present resources . Investigation of potential camera sites . Analysis of emergency service response times
Warning motorists approaching problem area	. Motorway warning displays . Roadside radio	. Investigation of information requirements . Investigation of potential warning devices . Analysis of accident types
Diversion of traffic from motorway to alternate surface routes	. Ramp metering . Advisory routing signs . Commercial radio . Roadside radio . Display terminals at major generators . Recorded phone messages	. Investigation of potential alternate routes . Analysis of corridor travel times . Analysis of corridor traffic volumes . Investigation of informational requirements . Investigation of potential devices and operation methodology
Accommodation of diverted traffic by surface roadways	. Direct control of signals adjacent to motorway . Provision of information to master traffic signal controller . Alternate route guidance	. Investigation of present and potential signal operations . Investigation of information transfer methodology . Analysis of roadway demand/capacity relationships . Area origin and destination patterns

IV.2.3. Environmental problems

The operation of all roadways are affected by weather and the other acts of nature. When it rains it lowers the coefficient of friction of the pavement which increases the chance for skidding accidents. Snow and cold weather often cause ice patches along the roadway which can become very hazardous. The evaluation of the effect of such occurrences can be determined from accident records of the roadways in the corridor. The weather is usually noted on accident forms so that the extent and location of problem areas can be determined. The types of problems and proposed evaluation studies involved for an area is provided in Table IV.3.

Table IV.3

INVESTIGATION OF ENVIRONMENTAL PROBLEMS

Problem	Potential Solutions	Evaluation Studies Proposed
Icy roadways	. Advanced warning signs or signals . Roadside radio	. Review of accident records . Review of weather experience . Investigation of automatic detection techniques
Fog and dust	. Warning beacons . Advanced warning signs or signals . Roadside radio	. Review of accident records . Analysis of fog experience . Analysis of dust storm experience
Sun glare	. Warning beacons	. Personal observation

IV.3 Analysis of Solutions

A meaningful analysis of corridor candidate systems requires that the goals be weighted numerically according to their relative importance. The degree of importance for the proposed facility should depend upon two factors:

- the merit, or desirability of having the goal achieved; and
- the extent to which the need is being met by the present facility.

The above analyses can only be made after the studies mentioned in Section IV.2 have been completed and the current and expected traffic problems discussed. Then the relative priorities or weights can be assigned to the goals based on a considerable amount of judgment on the part of the local officials who must eventually operate the system. The weight might be assigned by an advisory committee organised for the corridor project. An illustrative example of the outcome of such a procedure is presented in Table IV.4.

A matrix can be developed to express the relationship that exists between the functional subsystems and the systems goals. This matrix can show that each functional subsystem may contribute to more than one system goal and each system goal can be supported by more than one functional subsystem. A sample matrix which was developed for one such study is shown in Table IV.5. It should be realised that the numerical values are arbitrary and the analyst may wish to modify these values or develop his own weighting system.

The column entries in the matrix indicate the degree to which each of the functional subsystems supports the goal associated with the particular column. Each column will therefore have a sum of unity as shown on the matrix. The values contained in the matrix are based primarily on engineering judgment of the evaluation team. Then these data, combined with the relative priority weighting attached to the system goals by the advisory committee will form the basis for the evaluation of candidate systems.

IV.4 Documentation of Results

When the corridor control facility is installed, actual evaluation studies must be conducted to determine how effectively the system operates. It is most desirable to have data collected before and after the system is put in operation but in some cases, such data may not be comparable because of external influences. The data required for evaluating the problems, may provide an excellent basis to evaluate the effectiveness of the system when it is put in operation. The basic system measurements can be classified into four types of studies. These studies should consist of

Table IV.4

RELATIVE WEIGHTS ASSIGNED TO THE SYSTEM GOALS(1)

Goal	Weight
Reduce recurring motorway congestion	27
Improve merging operations	42
Reroute traffic around lane blockages	181
Prevent surface congestion from backing onto motorway	64
Advise drivers of motorway problems	147
Alert drivers at temporary hazard locations	135
Facilitate maintenance operations	47
Advise motorway drivers as to safe speed	
Provide service to troubled motorists	66
Expedite removal of lane blockages	140
Facilitate enforcement of traffic laws	129
	22
Total	1,000

1) Courage and Bissell, "Jones Falls Expressway Surveillance and Control System, A Preliminary Engineering Report" prepared for Baltimore, Maryland, June 1971.

. System operational measures (how well the equipment functions);
. System acceptance measures (how well drivers understand and accept information);
. System efficiency measures (how well corridor traffic flows); and,
. System safety measures (how well hazardous situations are reduced).

The overall evaluation of the traffic corridor, as stated before, is to determine, to the extent possible, how well the system objectives or goals are met, and what costs have been incurred to meet these goals.

IV.4.1 System operational measures

It is assumed that equipment and development records of costs will be maintained when the corridor control facility is being installed. Also records should be kept of actual system operational costs to compare the actual systems costs with the preliminary engineering estimates.

In addition to cost information, the actual system equipment operations should be monitored and recorded to note what, when, where and how a system control measure is activated. The actual implementation of a control measure, particularly when automatically displayed (such as a delay warning) should be checked in the field to ensure that the control function is actually desired and properly displayed. This will be particularly important during the initial three months that the system is put in operation.

Table IV.5

RELATIONSHIP BETWEEN FUNCTIONAL SUBSYSTEMS AND SYSTEM GOALS

Functional Subsystems	Reduce Recurring Motorway Congestion	Improve Merging Operations	Reroute Traffic Around Capacity Reductions	Prevent Surface Congestion from Backing onto Motorway	Advise Drivers of Motorway Problems	Alert Drivers at Temporary Hazard Locations	Facilitate Maintenance Operations	Advise Drivers on Motorway as to Safe Speed	Provide Service to Troubled Motorists	Expedite Removal of Capacity Reducing Incidents	Facilitate Enforcement of Traffic Laws
Ramp Access Controls	.90	1.00	.10								
Corridor Signal Controls			.20	.90							
Motorway Hazard Warnings						.80	.40				
Speed Reduction Warnings	.10				.20			.30			
Maintenance Warnings					.20		.30	.20			
Delay Warnings			.15		.20						
Environmental Warnings					.20		.10	.50			
Advisory Routing Messages			.30		.10						
Commercial Radio Messages			.20		.10						
Police Traffic Services			.05	.10		.10	.10		.20	.30	1.00
Motorway Patrol Services						.10	.10		.30	.40	
Motorist Aid Services									.50	.30	
Total	1.00	1.00	1.00	1.00	1.00	1.00	1.00	1.00	1.00	1.00	1.00

Actual records should be maintained on equipment performance to determine the life of hardware components. These records will aid in developing a preventive maintenance programme to minimise system breakdowns. The records should be maintained continously.

The actuation of the changeable message signs, roadside radio and other information systems should be checked weekly. The warning signals should be manually turned on and off in the control centre as an observer drives up and down the motorway reporting his observations to the control centre by radio voice communications. This should be co-ordinated with a weekly check of the emergency expressway telephone system.

The operation of the surface street alternate route signs should be checked weekly similar to the motorway information systems.

IV.4.2 System acceptance measures

Studies should be conducted to determine how the motorists accept and respond to the information and control measures (see Section III.5). These studies should be conducted after the system has been in operation for some time and the motorists have had a chance to become familiar with the various control messages. The studies should include:

Speed Studies to determine if motorists slow down when the changeable message signs display reduced speeds. This can be accomplished with radar speed meters or some other speed measuring device.

Surface Street Diversion Studies to determine if surface street drivers will use alternate routes when the alternate route corridor messages are activated. This can be accomplished through volume flow reductions measured by on-ramp detectors and machine counters placed along the alternate routes.

Motorway Diversion Studies to determine if motorists will leave the motorway when extensive delay ahead warnings are displayed. This can be measured by increased off ramp detectors counts.

Congestion Slowdown Studies to determine if drivers slow down in response to the warning signals before they approach the beginning of the congested queue. This can best be accomplished by moving vehicle studies in traffic or time-lapse TV or photography to measure rates of deceleration.

Motorist Questionnaire Survey to determine their understanding and opinion of the system. This can best be done by handing out mail-return questionnaires to motorists who use the system. This should be conducted 3 months or more after the system has been in operation, and repeat drivers have experienced situations where the corridor control system should have aided their travels.

IV.4.3 System efficiency measures

Studies should be conducted to evaluate the effectiveness of the surveillance and control system to improve the efficiency of traffic movement through the corridor. These studies should be conducted periodically, but these studies should be emphasized during the three months before the control system is turned on (while the surveillance system is operating) and then the three months following when both the control and the surveillance systems are in operation.

The following studies should be conducted:

Recurring Motorway Congestion should be studied to determine if any reductions occur in events such as the off-ramp traffic backing onto the motorway. These events can be measured by the off-ramp detectors and the occupancy rates of the sampling detectors directly upstream from the exit ramps.

The throughput of the corridor should be determined based on speed and delay surveys and traffic volume counts. The variance of travel times should be measured for day to day operations to indicate the predictability of expected travel times, and to determine usual travel time improvements which can be contributed to the new system being in operation.

From these speed and delay studies, etc., calculations can be made for estimates of energy saved due to reduced stop and go operations, air pollution emission improvements due to smoother flow operations, passenger hours saved due to improved travel times.

Non-recurring Motorway Congestion should be studied when an event is recorded. The system delay can be measured through the count station detectors. The amount of traffic diverted can be measured by the ramp detectors. Some measures of effect should be developed for the surface roadways which may best be done by conducting speed and delay runs on these highways during these events.

The amount of delay to the corridor traffic should be determined for similar types of incidents with and without the new system in operation. The capability of alternate routes to carry increased traffic loads due to diverted traffic must be periodically checked. The advice and information provided to motorists must be reviewed to ensure that credible messages are being provided.

Service times to troubled motorists should be recorded to determine system effects and improvements from the new system operations. This area of analysis is expected to be most difficult to evaluate as it is extremely rare that similar types of incidents occur at the same location and same traffic situation. Thus it may be impossible to make evaluations with and without the new system in operation. The analyses should be able to extrapolate the probable results that would have occurred if the system were not in operation from results of the system measurements when it is in operation.

IV.4.4 System safety measures

An important benefit to be expected is the reduction of certain types of accidents and the decreased response time to major incidents. Studies to measure these effects include:

Rear-end Collision accident statistics should be collected for a substantial period before and after the control system is implemented. It is expected that the speed controls and the warning signals should reduce the number of rear-end collisions.

Response Time Logs should be maintained for incidents detected by the motorway surveillance and control system. The time the incident is detected by the system should be noted and the time it is confirmed and aid is provided should also be recorded. Analyses can then be made on the effects provided by the control system.

Fixed Object Accidents may be indicated by an impact detection system under ex-perimentation in a number of countries. These systems will record when a vehicle has struck a guardrail, bridgerail or light pole. The response time to such accidents should be measured as it is expected to be substantially reduced par-ticularly during off-peak periods.

Merging Accident Records should be maintained to be able to evaluate the safety provided when ramp metering is in operation.

IV.5 Concluding Remarks

The assessment procedures for a corridor study should be an involved continuing process from the beginning of the system development to the end of its operation. It need not be done by one group, but it should be a co-ordinated effort among all involved agencies.

As more research is completed as suggested in Chapter VI of this report, the assess-ment of traffic corridor problems and potential solutions will be more reliable. The probable affects of individual system components should be known as well as the effects of combined system components should be documented.

V

APPROACHES TO ECONOMIC EVALUATION

V.1 Introduction

Economic evaluations are generally based on the comparison of present and future calculated benefits (or part of them) provided by the improvement considered with the expenditure (capital cost, maintenance and operation) involved in providing an electronic aid system for corridor traffic control.

The goal should be a system yielding the best return on the investment.

Obviously economic calculations for specific projects should be evaluated differently than those projects considered to serve also as an experimental facility. It should be noted that since corridor control constitutes an advanced traffic engineering technique, experimental projects may be implemented for other reasons than those merely concerned with concrete economic rentability.

It should also be considered that traffic corridor control investments which bring about improved level of service and safety in a corridor may also have an impact on the choice of route. However in the following, it is assumed that no farreaching changes regarding existing travel demand and pattern occur.

V.2 Cost Items

The costs should reflect the use of resources in the community. This means that specific taxes on vehicles, gasoline, etc. which should be regarded as payments from the private to the public sector, should not be considered as costs. In the framework of the economic theory this is only valid on the basis of the hypothesis of an economic evaluation from a community point of view.

If the traffic volumes generated were taken into account, it would be necessary to include individual costs (i.e. compromising specific taxes) in order to evaluate road user surplus. Taxes common to all capital assets should be included in costs if the investments in a highway electronic aid system are to be compared with investments in other public or private sectors.

When computing the cost of proposed equipment, it is essential that planning and design have reached such a stage that quantities can be reasonably estimated for each component. Estimates are necessary for each alternate design for which economic feasibility is to be analysed. Detailed analysis of the cost of each equipment component permits the consideration of different service lives and salvage values for each of them.

Annual maintenance and operating costs may be of importance in this case, and consequently must be estimated as best as possible.

Since the total number of factors affecting motor vehicles operating costs is great and their measurement difficult, it is desirable to classify the vehicles into groups and then determine the cost of operation of each group under specific conditions of use. Usually two or three groups are used as, for example, the following:

1. Passenger cars and light commercial vehicles
2. Heavy vehicles
    a) Single unit trucks
    b) Combination of vehicles
3. Buses

Other items should be considered which include the value of time for various vehicle types, occupational groups and trip purposes, as well as the economic value assigned to comfort and convenience.

If a significant reduction in accidents is assumed as a result of investments, accident costs with and without investments should also be calculated. This implies an evaluation of expected saving in lives and injuries. Property damages are usually included in vehicle maintencance costs, but they may be separately handled.

Annual costs for each alternative which normally should be considered are:
- Vehicle operating costs (fuel, oil, maintenance, depreciation and interests)
- Occupant time costs
- Accident costs
- Discomfort and inconvenience costs
- System maintenance and operating costs
- (Vehicle and passenger fares)

V.3 Annual Benefits

Benefits from an improvement in the transportation system have typically been derived from computing the reduction in operating costs attributed to travel over the proposed or new facility as compared to the same travel over the existing system. These benefits, as well as the costs, vary as a function of traffic volumes. Benefits in a given year are the difference between annual costs without investment and annual costs with investment, both in the year considered and discounted.

V.4 Practical Examples

V.4.1 Paris Corridor Control System

The objective of this example calculation, for the control system installed on the A6-B6-C6 corridor for inbound traffic from the south of Paris, was to determine the minimum benefit needed to justify the installation of control system equipment.

The input data were the following:
- Total cost of the pilot system based on 1975 prices: \$6,150,000
- Total estimated traffic flow during one year: 2×10^7 vehicles
- Estimated Time cost (at the beginning of 1975): \$4.50/hour

If the system is to be amortized within $\underline{n}$ years (after the beginning of 1975) and disregarding the rate of interest, the minimum cost per vehicle will be

$$\frac{6,15 \times 10^6}{2 \times 10^7 \times n}$$

The corresponding time which must be saved as a result of the installation of the new system is

$$\frac{6,15 \times 10^6}{2 \times 10^7 \times n} \times \frac{3600}{4,50} \text{ seconds or } \frac{250}{n} \text{ seconds per vehicle.}$$

Table V.1

COSTS ASSOCIATED WITH MOTORWAY RAMP METERING SYSTEMS (IN DOLLARS)

Project	Number of ramps	Capital and installation costs							Amortized cost per ramp (see note 2) (annual)	Annual cost (per ramp)			Year
		Subunit costs (per system)					Total cost per						
		Detection equipment	Ramp signals	Telemetry	Computer control	Other (see notes)	System	Ramp		Maintenance	Operation	Total	
I. ACTUAL SCHEMES													
1. Atlanta	3		6,750				$6,750	$2,250	350	100	50	500	1968
2. Minnesota	2		4,200				4,200	2,100	300	200	50	550	1970
3. Los Angeles(1) (Habour Motorway, fixed time)	6		40,000				40,000	6,650	1,000	n.a.	n.a.	n.a.	1968
4. Detroit (Texas Transportation Institute)	8	24,800	19,200	16,000	160,000		220,000	27,500	4,100	1,100	1,000	6,200	1968
5. Chicago(2)	8				359,000			15,500	2,300	1,200	600	4,100	1971
6. Houston (Local digital - gap acceptance only)	8	20,000			68,000		88,000	11,000	1,650	200	1,250	3,100	1970
7. Houston (Local digital - full control)	8	45,000			95,700		140,700	17,600	2,600	500	1,250	4,350	1970
8. Houston (Central digital - full control)	8	37,000		13,200	128,500		178,700	22,350	3,350	500	1,250	5,100	1970
9. Dallas	39	143,300	113,950	214,400	244,400		716,050	18,350	2,750	750	250	3,750	1971
II. PROPOSED SCHEMES													
1. Los Angeles(3)(Surveillance and control)	9	72,000		165,000			237,000	26,350	3,950	1,400	900	6,250	1971
2. Baltimore(4)(Jones-Falls Expressway)	12	30,000	36,000	108,000	39,200		213,200	17,800	2,650	1,000	200	3,850	1971

1) Includes extensive restriping of ramps.
2) Computer purchased in 1969 for surveillance on many expressways.
3) Estimate includes extensive surveillance of Harbour Motorway - leg of 42-mile surveillance project, and control of 9 ramps on the southbound Harbour Motorway.
4) Project proposes the use of a larger computer involved in traffic signal control of city streets for detector surveillance.
5) See text for discussion.

NOTES:
1. n.a. means not available.
2. All capital and installation costs amortized over 10 years at an 8 per cent interest rate.
3. Annual operating cost is exclusive of salaries except where stated and largely consists of power and telephone charges. 4. All entries rounded to nearest $50.

V.4.2 Ramp Control Systems in the United States

Table V.1 shows actual costs of motorway control systems for nine projects and estimated figures on three projects within the United States, obtained from data published in 1972(1). In the table, the three first projects are fixed time systems and the others, except the last one, are traffic responsive systems. The following general conclusions can be drawn:

- the number of ramps has an important bearing on the cost per ramp, since some costs, for example, computer control, do not increase proportionally with the number of ramps added to the system;
- where extensive motorway surveillance is employed for other reasons such as incident detection, there is usually more surveillance than is necessary for ramp control alone, and obviously the cost per ramp is somewhat higher.

The benefits that have been achieved in the actual operating of ramp-metering projects are summarised in Table V.2. The figures in this table should be viewed as order-of-magnitude estimates only.

In Table V.3 are tabulated the benefits and costs for eight operating systems in the United States and the corresponding benefit-cost ratios. Although it should be noted that the operating costs do not seem to fully relect the personnel costs, the following general conclusions can be drawn from this table:

- Since all projects have a ratio greater than unity, they are all considered economically beneficial to the community.
- All projects compare favourably with highway improvement schemes that often have benefit-cost ratios in the range 1-3.

V.5 Concluding Remarks

The approach of the economic evaluation process cannot rely solely on the classical benefit/cost type of studies. It is most difficult to assign monetary values to many of the anticipated results listed in the corridor control goals. The value of travel time, and motorist comfort; the reduction of air pollution and the savings in fuel consumption; the reduction in motorist service times, and even the costs of accidents are most difficult to convert into acceptable monetary terms. At this point in time it is not necessarily required that a high benefit/cost ratio exist for systems designed to aid the travelling public. Such programmes as highway beautification and roadway safety do not consider the need for a high monetary rate-of-return for the costs incurred; therefore, it should not be required that the corridor facility be evaluated only in this light.

Until recently the development of public facilities was primarily limited by the avilability of funds. However, in response to growing concerns over environmental issues, social impacts, fuel conservation, etc., an increasing emphasis is being placed upon the maximum utilisation of existing facilities rather than the construction of new or redundant facilities, particularly in the more developed countries.

---

1) P. F. Everall: "Urban Freeway Surveillance and Control", Federal Highway Administration, 1972.

Table V.2

BENEFITS ACHIEVED IN RAMP METERING PROJECTS

Location	Number of ramps used in evaluation	Travel time Change(1) (Vehicle-hours per year)	Travel time Annual value ($)	Accidents Change per year(1)	Accidents Annual value ($)	Other effects of ramp metering	Assumptions made	Annual net benefit per system ($)
Atlanta	1	+8,200	-24,600	-70	+49,000	Metering caused motorists to divert to upstream ramps, but also caused overall increase in motorway use.	Ramp vehicles delayed 1 extra minute by metering. Diverted vehicles delayed 2 extra minutes by metering. 250 working days per year.	+24,000
Minnesota	2	+5,640	+16,900	n.a.	-	Corridor throughput unchanged. Slight reduction in alternative route travel times.	130 dry working days per year. No benefits on wet days.	+16,900
Los Angeles	6	-108,300	+325,000	n.a.	-	Additional benefits through increased driver satisfaction, less frustration, etc.	130 incident-free p.m. peak periods per year. No benefits on days on which incidents occur.	+325,000
Detroit (Texas Transportation Institute)	8	-225,000	+675,000	n.a.	-	High meter violation rate in this project.	250 working days per year. Conservative estimate since benefits of traffic-responsive metering greater on incident days.	+675,000
Chicago (outbound Eisenhower Expressway)	8	-64,000	+192,000	-51	+39,300	Some permanent diversion to alternative routes.	250 days on which benefits achieved. Conservative estimate since traffic-responsive metering more beneficial on incident days.	+231,300
Houston (gap acceptance only)	8	-51,300	+153,900	-33	+19,800	Reduction in vehicle operating costs = $16,400. Level of service qualitative benefits also.	—	+190,000
Houston (full control)	8	-72,670	+218,000	-40	+24,000	Reduction in vehicle operating costs = $18,400. Level of service qualitative benefits also.	—	

1) + = Increase
   - = Decrease

2) + = Savings
   - = Disbenefits.

3. Values of accidents used are:
   Atlanta - $700 per urban reported property damage only accident.
   Chicago - $770 per urban motorway passenger car accident.
   Houston - $600 per accident.

NOTES
1. n.a. in this table means not available.
2. Value of time of $3 per vehicle-hour is used throughout.

50

The methodology proposed to evaluate a corridor is based on measuring all facets of the installation and operation of the control system that can be realistically quantified followed by a variety of system evaluation calculations. Cost-effectiveness taken in conjunction with the other considerations, as discussed in Chapter IV, provides as rational a basis as can be expected for economic valuation purposes.

Table V.3

A COMPARISON OF SYSTEM COSTS AND BENEFITS

Location	Number of ramps	Annual net benefit	Equivalent uniform annual cost	Benefit/cost ratio
Atlanta	1	$24,400	$500	49
Minnesota	2	16,900	1,100	15
Los Angeles	6	325,000	7,200(1)	45
Detroit	8	675,000	49,600	14
Chicago	8	231,300	32,800	7.1
Houston (local digital-gap acceptance only)	8	190,100	24,800	7.7
Houston (local digital - full control)	8	260,400	34,800	7.5
Houston (central digital - full control)	8	260,400	40,800	6.4

1) Annual maintenance and operating costs estimated to be $200 per ramp.

VI

RESEARCH NEEDS

The main priority research areas in corridor control are:
- incident management;
- short-term prediction;
- strategies;
- assessment methods;
- driver communication techniques.

VI.1 Incident Management

Automatic incident detection is part of a total traffic incident management system. The problems in testing incident detection strategies cannot be solved without considering the hardware problems.

The main problems for further research are:

1. Criteria for installing an automatic detection system in place of the present methods, on the basis of cost considerations, accident rates and the speed with which the rest of the system can respond.
2. Choice of traffic parameters (or combinations) to be observed in detecting traffic incidents.
3. In general, development of inexpensive and reliable systems (with acceptable response times) for detection of traffic incidents; in particular, development of appropriate traffic detectors and investigation on the optimal configuration for and spacings of these detectors.
4. Studies regarding methods and regulations to reach the incident locations quickly and studies regarding optimum incident clearance procedures.
5. Development and testing of reliable detectors (high detection and small false alarm rates) indicating special meteorological conditions, especially the prediction of ice formation and fog.

VI.2 Short-Term Prediction

Short-term prediction is used in traffic control as well as incident detection. The main needs for research in this area are:

1. Study of the amount and accuracy of data required relative to proposed strategies; investigations of methods of collecting traffic flow data including the study of data needs for traffic corridor control.
2. Validation and continued development of techniques for updating the origin-destination pattern from measured flows.

3. Development of methods for predicting short-term vehicle arrival rates for optimum traffic operation; including investigation of modes of prediction (e.g. one-minute flows, historical data), automatic measurements, data analysis, estimation of errors.

VI.3 Strategies

Criteria for corridor control may differ depending on the traffic condition and the control policy. Criteria might be altered even for a single system depending on the prevailing traffic conditions.

The range of research needs in this area is extensive. There appears to be a set of general research needs as well as specific research problem areas common to each of these needs.

The strategies for corridor traffic control must include explicit consideration of traffic safety, travel time, energy consumption, and environmental implications as a basis for selection.

The general research needs are:

1. Continued development of theoretical corridor traffic control strategies.
2. Further development, particularly with a view to practical implementation, of existing theoretical strategies, using historical data and real time information.
3. Development of simulation techniques for study and evaluation of possible strategies.
4. Development of operational corridor traffic control strategies.

The specific research problem areas of particular interest are:

5. Determination of optimum diversion strategies at special sections with a specific aim, such as traffic safety, energy consumption and environmental factors.
6. Study of optimum ramp closure policies along a corridor.
7. Optimum procedures for determining mandatory or advisory speeds.
8. Development of queue detection and warning strategies.

Although the report does not include discussions of public transport and parking, their effects on corridor traffic control should be investigated.

VI.4 Assessment Methods

Special attention has to be given to the methods for evaluating the various types of corridor control. The following studies appear to have first priority:

1. Development of methods for testing incident detection strategies.
2. Development of simple methods for the evaluation of traffic flow.
3. Testing of the various strategies by comparative theoretical and practical evaluation.
4. Development of additional methods for measuring the effectiveness of corridor control.
5. Cost-benefit-analysis of the various types of corridor control.

VI.5 Driver Communication Techniques

The Group recognises the importance of co-operative research in the area of large scale driver information and communication systems, especially on the software aspects. The communication techniques are being studied in depth by COST Group 30. The following areas are considered to be of special interest:

1. Studies about the optimum signing and signalling for informing the drivers on certain conditions such as driving hazards, delays etc.

2. Investigations about driver's reaction to and confidence in different symbols or messages for advice or instruction.
3. Finding and testing simple and reliable systems to give messages to drivers containing quantitative informations.
4. Investigations about needed data for in-vehicle aural and visual communication and guidance.
5. Investigations of the effectiveness of driver communication systems.

KEY REFERENCES

1. Beckmann, H.; Jacobs, F.; Lenz, K.H.; Wiedemann, R.; Zackor, H., Das Fundamental-diagramm - Eine Zusammenstellung bisheriger Ergebnisse, Forschungsarbeiten aus dem Strassenwesen, Heft 89, 1973.

2. Behrendt, J., Entwicklungen zur Verkehrslenkung auf Autobahnen VDI-Bildungswerk (BW 1870), 1971.

3. Bundesministers für Verkehr, Einsatz eines Steuerungsmodells zur Verkehrsstromführung mit Hilfe von Weckselwegweisern, Forschungsauftrag 3.017 G 74 I (1974).

4. Bundesminister für Verkehr, Verkehr auf den Bundesautobahnen 1967, 1968,...1973 Ergebnisse der Verkehrszählung mit automatischen Zählgeräten.

5. Bundesminister für Verkehr, Verkehrsbeeinflussende Massnahmen im Rahmen des deutschen Korridorexperiments, Forschungsauftrag 3.033 R 74 I (1974).

6. Boesefeldt, J.; Keudel, K., Möglichkeiten verkehrsabhängiger Massnahmen auf Schnell-strassen, Strassenbau und Strassenverkehrstechnik, Heft 128, 1972.

7. Busch, F., Verkehrsbeeinflussung auf Bundesautobahnen Ein Rahmenplan des Bundes-ministers für Verkehr, Strasse und Autobahn 22, Heft 9, 1971.

8. Concannon, P., McCabe, L., and Ricci, R., Urban Traffic Corridor Study, U.S. Department of Transportation, Transportation Systems Centre, January 1974 (relating to development of SCOT Model).

9. Courage K., and Bissell, H., "Recording and Analysis of Traffic Engineering Measures" Highway Research Record 398, Highway Research Board, Washington, D.C. 1972.

10. Everall, Paul, Urban Freeway Surveillance and Control The State of the Art, Revised Edition June 1973, U.S. Department of Transportation, Federal Highway Administration.

11. Everts, K.; Spies, G.; Thomas, K.B., Verkehrsbeeinflussung auf Bundesautobahnen durch Wechselwegweisung, Entwicklung einer Konzeption für den Versuchsbereich Rhein-Main, Untersuchung des Autobahnamtes Frankfurt, Mai 1972

12. Everts, K.; Zackor, H., Untersuchung von Steuerungsmodellen zur Verkehrsstrom-führung mit Hilfe von Weckselwegweisern, Bericht zum Forschungsauftrag 10.29 (1972) des Bundesminister für Verkehr, Abschluss 1974.

13. Gottardi, G., Anschlusssteuerung an der Nationalstrasse N 3 in Zürich; Zürich Veröffentlicht in "Strasse und Verkehr", Nr. 12/1970.

14. Henry, Laurens, and Libertalis, Régulation du complexe A6-H6; Etude de principe : IRT-1969; Communication au Symposium International de Versailles : Juin 1970.

15. Hoppe, K., und Vincent, R.A., Bevorzugung des öffentlichen Verkehrs in lichtsignal-geregelten Verkehrsnetzen. ("Public Transport Priority at signal controlled Net-works") Veröffent licht in "UTIP-Revue", Vol. 21-4/1972.

16. I.R.T., Le programme AFRODIT (Affectation et Régulation optimale d'itineraires), June, 1971.

17. I.R.T., Régulation de la Sortie SI du M.I.N. de Rungis sur l'autoroute A6 (étude experimentale), March, 1970.

18. Knoll, E.; Ullrich, J., Verkehrsbeeinflussung durch Wechselverkehrszeichen, Wechsel-Wegweisung, Busspuren und Richtgeschwindigkeiten - Erfahrungen in Hessen, Hessischer Minister für Wirtschaft und Technik, Wiesbaden, o.J. (1972).

19. Krell, K., Möglichkeiten und Grenzen kybernetischer Hilfen, Strasse und Autobahn, 23, Heft 4, 1972.

20. Krell, K., "Probleme der Korridorsteuerung", Strassenverkehrstechnik, 1975, Heft 7.

21. Krell, K., "Probleme der Sicherheitstechnik im Strassenwesen", Zeitschrift für Verkehrssicherheit, (20) 1974, Heft 1, S.21-45.

22. Krell, K., "Verbesserung der Flüssigkeit des Verkehrs durch Verkehrslenkung", Die Polizei, 1971, Heft 3, S.80-86.

23. Laurens, Le viaduc de Plombières, à Marseilles : contrôle d'accès et de détection automatique d'incidents. Transport - Environment - Circulation n°4 : Avril-Mai 1974.

24. Le Pera, R. and Nenzi, R., The Naples Tollway Computer System for Highway Surveillance and Control, Reprints of the 2nd IFAC/IFIP/IFORS Symposium, Monte-Carlo, 1974, North Holland/American Elsevier Pub.

25. Le Pera, R. and Nenzi, R., TANA - An Operating Surveillance System for Highway Traffic Control, Proc. of the IEEE, Vol. 61, No. 5, May 1973.

26. Lemaître et Laurand, "Signalisation d'exploitation et de sécurité sur les autoroutes péri-urbaines," Communication au Symposium de Monté-Carlo, September 1974.

27. Leygue, F., "Relations vitesse - débis sur autoroute," IRT, - November 1966.

28. Maloney, M.F., Lindberg, H., and Cleven, G., "A Solution to Intercity Traffic Corridor Problems?", Public Roads, Volume 37, No. 5, U.S. Department of Transportation, Federal Highway Administration, June 1973.

29. Nenzi, R., and Anglisani, G., "Real Time Computer System Controls and Naples Tollway," Traffic Engineering and Control, Vol. 15, No. 10/11 Feb./Mar. 74.

30. Nicolle, "La régulation de vitesse sur l'autoroute du Sud," IRT, Juillet, 1973.

31. SETRA, Directives pour la conception des opérations corridor (guide de programmation) Edition provisoire, August, 1974.

32. SETRA, Dossier-modèle d'études globales d'une opération corridor en France, du corridor Sud de LILLE, (en cours - achèvement fin 1er trimestre 1975 - version provisoire disponible).

33. SETRA, Généralités sur la méthodologie des opérations corridors en France (édition provisoire Décembre 1974).

34. SETRA, La signalisation des opérations d'exploitation en France : en rase campagne, dans les corridors urbains. (en cours - achèvement fin 2ème trimestre 1975 - version provisoire disponible).

35. SETRA, "Methodologie des opérations corridors en France", Guide de Programmation, (edition provisoire Décembre 1974).

36. Spring, A., Verkehrsabhängige Autobahnsteurerung, Stand der Forschungsarbeiten und Vorschläge für weitere Forschungen in der Schweiz, Ergebniss einer Umfrage in der Vereinigung Schweizerischer Verkehrsingenieure, August 1974.

37. Traffic Control Systems Handbook, to be published by U.S. Department of Transportation, Federal Highway Administration in 1975.

38. Thomas, K.B., Zur Systematik mechanischer Wechselverkehrszeichengeber (WZG), Strassenverkehrstechnik 15, Heft 6, 1971.

39. Vereinigug Schweizerischer Verkehrsingenieure, Autobahnanschlusssteuerung/koordinierte Stadtverkehrsregelung, Schlussbericht zu einem Forschungsauftrag to be published in 1975.

40. Vonhoff, H.J., Beschreibung von Einrichtungen zum Betrieb von Wechselverkehrszeichen, verkehrstechnische Auswirkungen und Einsatzmöglichkeiten, Forschungsgesellschaft für das Strassenwesen e.V., Köln Bericht zum Forschungsauftrag IV/118 (1970).

ANNEXES

1. PROCEDURES FOR INTERNATIONAL CO-OPERATIVE RESEARCH ON TRAFFIC CORRIDOR CONTROL.
2. INVENTORY OF EXPERIMENTAL CORRIDOR FACILITIES.
3. CONTROL MODELS USING THE DENSITY WAVE CONCEPT.
4. CONTROL MODELS USING THE CRITICAL QUEUE CONCEPT.
5. CONTROL MODELS BASED ON LINEAR PROGRAMMING.
6. AUTOMATIC INCIDENT DETECTION MODEL BASED ON OCCUPANCY PARAMETERS.
7. STATISTICAL INFORMATION ON MOTORWAY CLOSURES IN ENGLAND.
8. TYPES OF VARIABLE MESSAGE SIGNS.

Annex I

PROCEDURES FOR INTERNATIONAL CO-OPERATIVE
RESEARCH ON TRAFFIC CORRIDOR CONTROL

At its second meeting held in Zürich, Switzerland, on 16th and 17th December, 1971, the OECD Road Research Group T9 "International Corridor Experiment (ICE)" was informed of the decisions taken by the OECD Steering Committee for Road Research at their seventh session held on 1st and 2nd December, 1971, regarding the ICE work programme:

Considering the importance of traffic corridor research for future generalised traffic control;

Having regard to the high investments needed for traffic corridor facilities, the limited number of present and planned national traffic corridor projects in Member countries, and the considerable funds needed for research and development in this area;

Recognising the value, for all Member countries, of co-operative research work in the field of traffic corridor control, the aim being to optimise scarce national research resources and also to optimise the use and operation of present and planned national traffic corridor facilities;

Adopted the following procedures for international co-operative research on traffic corridor control.

OBJECTIVE

The purpose of an International Corridor Experiment is to develop and test strategies for the best operation of different types of freeway corridors. It is proposed that co-operative research can be conducted on a facility of a Member country on the basis of the research needs of another Member country.

POLICIES

In order to conduct a research experiment on the facilities of one country to meet the requirements of another OECD Member country, basic policies must be established and observed. These proposed policies are as follows:

1. A proposed traffic corridor research experiment must meet with the approval of the "host" country whose facilities will be used.
2. Any special equipment and/or personnel required to conduct the experiment will normally be furnished by the "guest" country.
3. No actual funds will normally be exchanged between countries.
4. The strategies, methods, procedures and experimental results must be reported to all OECD Member countries.

PROCEDURES

It is expected that a few basic procedures will be followed in initiating and conducting co-operative research experiments. These procedures are as follows:

1. An up-to-date inventory of all prospective traffic corridor facilities will be furnished to each OECD Member country each year by the Secretariat.

2. A proposed traffic corridor research experiment by a Member country will be sent to both the Secretariat and the representative of the country whose facilities may be used.

3. The proposed research project requirements must be mutually agreeable to both the countries involved and the specific details will be developed by the countries' representatives.

4. The detailed design of the experiment will be presented to and discussed by the Group.

5. When the experiment is conducted, the research results must be reported to all OECD Member representatives.

Annex 2

<u>INVENTORY OF EXPERIMENTAL</u>
<u>CORRIDOR FACILITIES</u>

FRANCE: CORRIDOR A6-B6-C6: Paris-Orly (South of Paris)

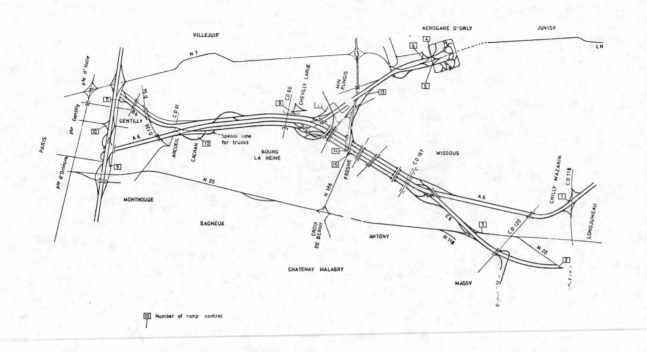

Type: 3 motorways linked with 2 signal controlled national roads.

Scope: Length: 12 km. Width: 3 km.

Strategy: Minimisation of overall journey time through maximisation of the number of
vehicles admitted to the motorway system.

System functions and/or control measure

- Predictive information about traffic conditions on
  the motorway at entrance points of system
- Prevention of oversaturation on motorways and diversion of motorway traffic (optimal distribution
  of demand according to available capacity)

- Variable assignment of motorway lanes to merging and
  diverging traffic
- Prevention of incidents and smoothing of traffic
  flow on the motorway to increase throughput

- Bus priority on entrance ramps
- Preferential treatment of truck traffic leaving
  Paris

Communication means

- Variable message signs (free,
  controlled, closed)
- Ramp control signals; variable
  directional signs and adequate
  co-ordination of traffic signals on National roads
- Optical signs for lane control

- Signs for variable speed limits;
  warning signs (accidents,
  bottlenecks, ice)
- Special access lanes for buses
- Reserved lanes for trucks

Detection of:

- Queues
- Volume

- Presence of cars on on-ramps
- Saturation by measuring occupancy
- Speed on A6
- Trucks

Overall observation

Detection means

- Inductive loops at 15 points
- 144 detectors at all entrances
  and exits and at some places
  inside the network
- 15 detectors
- 85 detectors
- 18 detectors
- 21 detectors

TV cameras

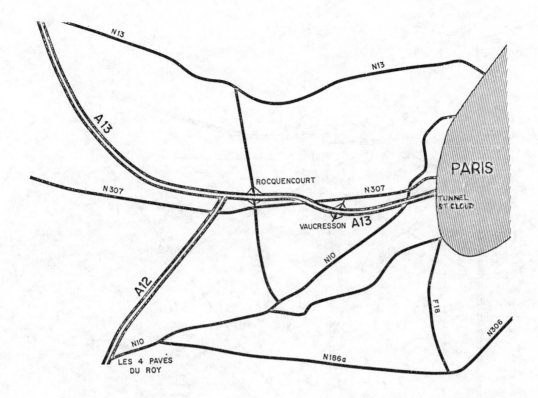

Type: 2 motorways with a common section of 10 km connected with 6 signal controlled National roads (80 controlled intersections).

Scope: Length: 20 km.   Width: 6 - 12 km.

Strategy: Minimisation of the overall journey time for the different directions according to the offered capacity of the different routes. Maximisation of the traffic flow on the motorway by lane control.

System functions and/or control measure

- Predictive information about traffic conditions on the motorways

- Prevention of oversaturation on motorways and diversion of motorway traffic (optimal distribution of demand according to available capacity)

- Variable assignment of motorway lanes to merging and diverging traffic and countermeasures for obstructed lanes
- Prevention of incidents and smoothing of traffic flow in order to increase throughput on the motorways

Detection of:

- Queues

- Volume

- Speed on the motorways
- Presence of cars on on-ramps
- Detection of accidents

- Ice and rain (in a later stage)

Communication means

- Variable message signs (free, controlled, closed) (gantries in 500 m distance on the motorway)
- Ramp control signals at 5 on-ramps; variable directional signs and adequate co-ordination of traffic signals on National roads
- Signals (red cross and green arrow) for lane control

- Signs for variable speed limits

Detection means

- Automatic detectors on the motorways and the National roads
- Automatic detectors on the motorways and the National roads
- Automatic detectors
- loop detectors
- Seismic detectors (for experimental purposes)
- Special detectors

FRANCE: CORRIDOR A1 Paris-Le Bourget - Roissy en France (North of Paris)

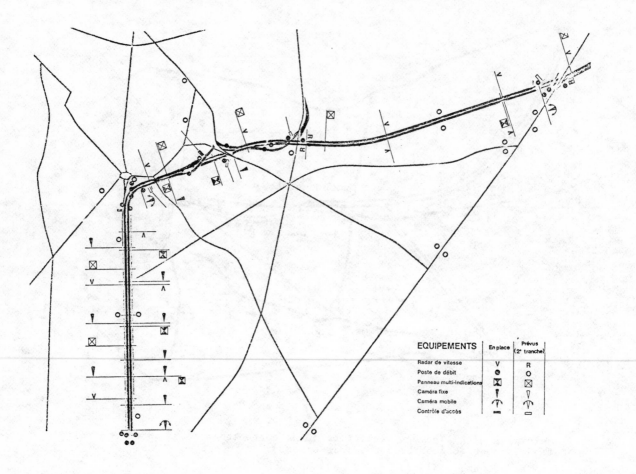

EQUIPEMENTS

	En place	Prévus (2ᵉ tranche)
Radar de vitesse	V	R
Poste de débit	●	O
Panneau multi-indications	⊠	⊠
Caméra fixe	▼	▽
Caméra mobile	⊤	⊤
Contrôle d'accès	▬	▭

Type: One motorway (2 x 4 lanes) connected with four National Roads.
Scope: Length 9 km.   Width 4 km.
Strategy: Prevention of oversaturation and incidents on the motorway.

System function and/or control measure

- Prevention of oversaturation on motorway

- Prevention of incidents on the motorway

Communication means

- Ramp control signals on access ramps
- Matrix warning signs (Accident, Fog, Ice, Works, Bottleneck, Slippery Road, etc.)
- Signals (red cross and green arrow) for lane control)

Detection of:

- Volume
- Speed

Overall observation

Detection means

- Loop detectors
- Radar detectors
- TV cameras

FRANCE: CORRIDOR A7/A51 North of Marseille

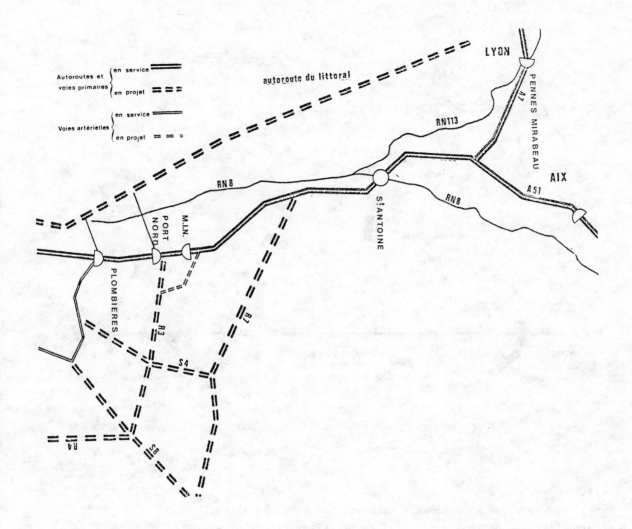

Type: One motorway (2 x 3 lanes) linked with one parallel National road

Scope: Length: 10 km.   Width: 4 km.

Strategy: Prevention of incidents and oversaturation on the motorway.

System function and/or control measures

- Prevention of oversaturation on motorway

- Prevention of incidents and smoothing of traffic flow in order to increase throughput on the motorway

Detection of:

- Length of vehicles
- Speeds
- Density
Overall observation

Communication means

- Control signals on access ramps; variable directional signs for diversion
- Signs for variable speed limits
- Signals for lane control

Detection means

- Radar detectors every 500 m

- TV cameras

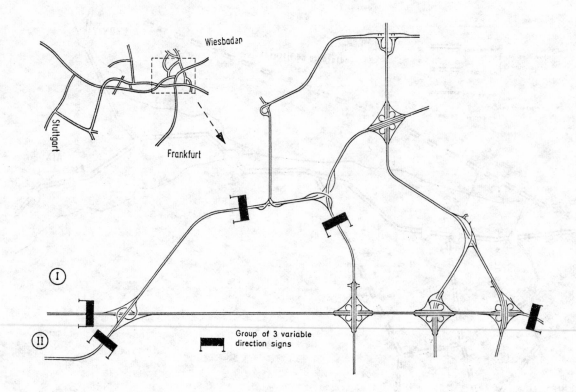

Type: Three parallel motorways connected by motorway links.

Scope: Length: 30 km   Width: 15 km.5. (First stage of a projected 30 km.
         Corridor Frankfurt (M) - Stuttgart).

Strategy: Maximisation of throughput, keeping traffic flowing by optimal diversion
          in cases of exceptionally high demand and for temporary capacity restraint.

System function and/or control measure	Communication means
- Predictive information on traffic conditions on the motorway before entering the corridor - Optimal diversion according to available capacity of different motorways	- Radio - Variable directional signs (example - sign positioning and sign faces - see figure on next page)

Detection of:	Detection means
- Volume - Speed - Occupancy - Incidents	- Loop detectors in interchange areas - patrols - TV cameras

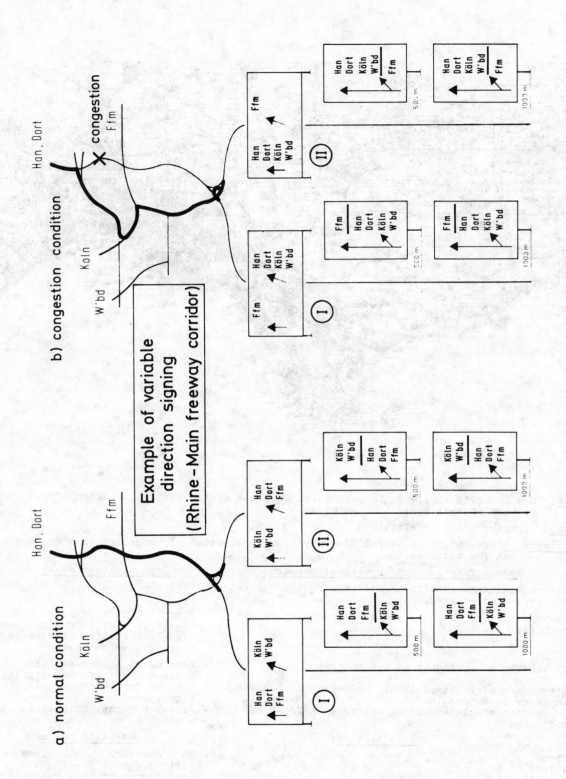

Example of variable direction signing (Rhine-Main freeway corridor)

a) normal condition

b) congestion condition

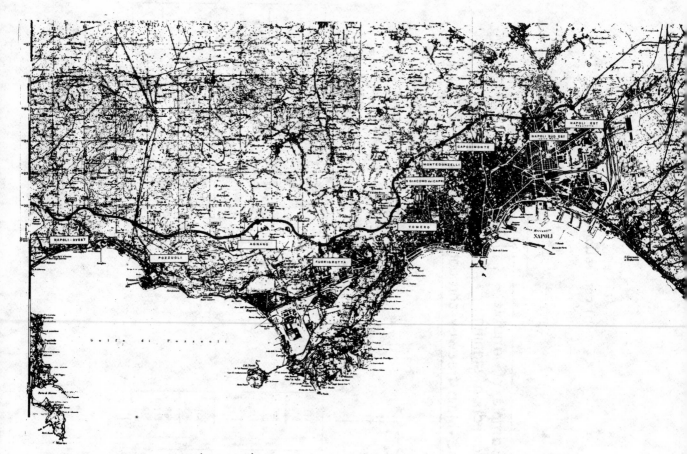

<u>Type</u>:   One motorway (tollway) in connection with the signal controlled urban street-
network of West Naples.

<u>Scope</u>:   Length: 14 km   Width: 3 km.

<u>Strategy</u>:   Minimisation of overall journey time, prevention of congestion and accidents
on the motorway.

<u>System function and/or control measure</u>	<u>Communication means</u>
- Information about traffic conditions on the motorway and beyond the exit-ramps	- Variable signs
- Prevention of oversaturation and congestion on the motorway	- Ramp control signals at 5 on-ramps. Variable directional signs for guiding drivers to appropriate toll gates
- Prevention of accidents on the motorway	- Warning signs (congestion, accident, bad weather conditions)
- Prevention of intolerable air pollution in tunnels in cases of congestion	- Signals for temporary closure of tunnels
- Prevention of queues on the motorway in front of exit ramps	- Variable signs indicating the closure of exit ramps

<u>Detection of</u>:	<u>Detection means</u>
- Speed - Volume - Density - Incidents - Queues on exit ramps - Presence of vehicles at on-ramps - Weather conditions	- 502 detectors on all lanes in distances of 125 - 250 m. (see figure on next page) - 82 loop detectors on the ramps - special detectors

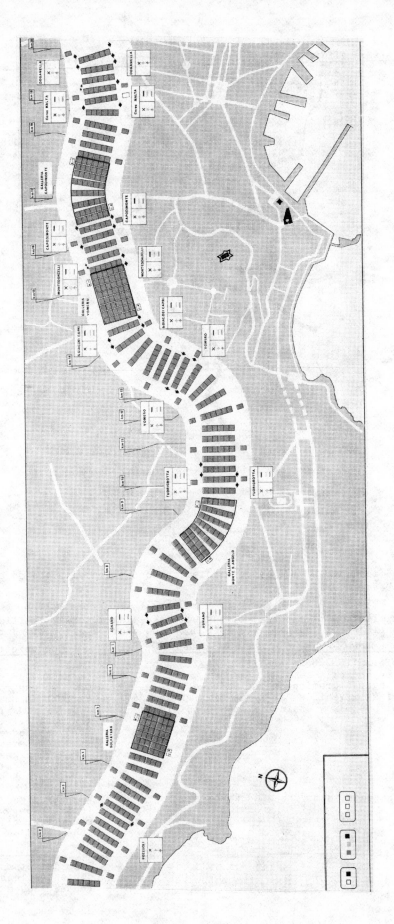

69

JAPAN: TOKYO METROPOLITAN EXPRESSWAY TOLLWAY Corridor System

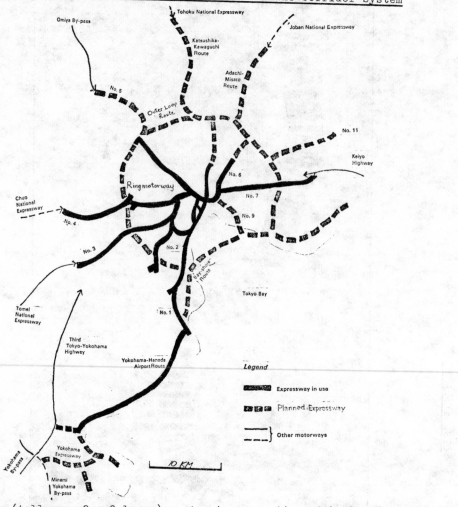

Type: Motorway (tollway - 2 x 2 lanes) system in connection with the adjacent signal controlled urban street network.

Scope: 100 km motorway-system, urban street network of 15 km radius.

Strategy: Maximisation of motorway throughput. Keeping motorway traffic flowing. Ensuring that journey time does not rise above a given standard level.

System functions and/or control measures

- Predictive information about traffic conditions on the motorway and beyond exit ramps
- Prevention of oversaturation on the motorway.
- Prohibition of slow vehicles at times of high demand or vehicles without snow chains in snow conditions

- Prevention of accidents on the motorway system

Communication means

- Radio & variable message signs (matrix type see fig. next page)
- On-ramp control by toll gates
- Variable message signs (matrix type) giving information about the possibilities of entrance to the motorway (ramp X open, ramp Y metered, ramp Z closed)
- Variable signs. Temporarily closed for "slow vehicles of type....." "Only vehicles fitted with snow chains permitted".
- Warning signs (matrix type) (congestion, works, accident, snow, ice, slippery road surface, etc.)

Detection of:

- volume
- speed
- occupancy

Overall observation

Detection means

- Loop detectors in all lanes in distances less than 500 m (ring route) 1000 m (radial routes)

- 82 TV cameras

Panneaux variables (matrices) sur l'autoroute
Matrix Type Variable Message Signs on the Expressway

|←————— 5.300 km —————→|

Exemples de messages
Examples of Messages

Condition de circulation / Traffic Condition

銀	座		方	面		渋	滞	2	km

Bouchon de 2 KM en direction de Ginza
Ginza Direction Congestion Length 2 KM

Accident

江	戸	橋	事	故		不	通	

Edobashi Obstruction par cause d'accident
Edobashi Accident Blocked

Regulation

料	金	所	流	入	制	限	中	

Trafic d'entrée limité aux postes de péage
Tollgate Incoming Flow Restricted

					通	行	止	

Route fermée
Road Closed

Avertissement / Warning

					ス	リ	ッ	プ	注	意

Attention route glissante
Slip Caution

NETHERLANDS: CORRIDOR N13/N12: The Hague - Rotterdam

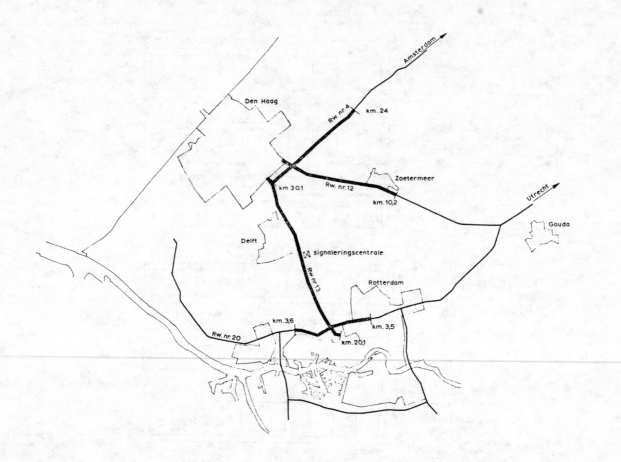

Type: Motorway connecting two signal controlled urban street networks.

Scope: Length: 30 km motorway.

Strategy: Prevention of incidents on the motorway, harmonisation of motorway-control and signal control of street networks.

System functions and/or control measures

- Prevention of incidents and smoothing of the traffic flow in order to increase throughput on the motorway

- Diversion of traffic from affected lanes

- Aid for traffic entering the motorway

Communication means

- Signs for indication of variable speed limits. Flashing amber lights for warning against hazardous conditions
- lane control signs (red cross)
- all signs of U.K. matrix type

Detection of:

- volume
- speed
- occupancy
- weather conditions

Detection means

- inductive loops

- special detectors

- patrols

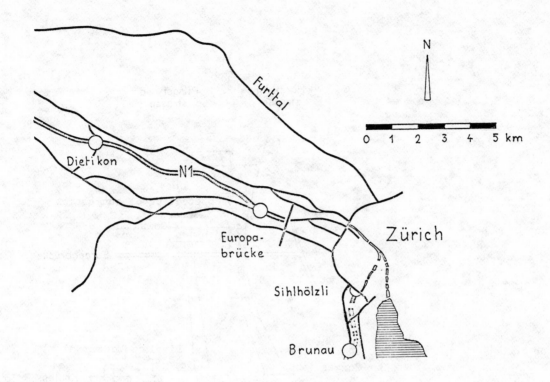

Type: One motorway leading to the signal controlled urban street network.

Scope: Length: 11 km motorway.

Strategy: Diversion of motorway traffic in cases of congestion on last Section of the motorway. Prevention of rear-end accidents.

System functions and/or control measures	Communication means
- Diversion of traffic to Zürich from the motorway and control of entering motorway traffic	- Variable lane closure and directional signs (see figures on next page) (advisory, or (if the motorway is blocked), mandatory).
	- Signs showing "motorway closed" or "Attention" in front of on-ramps
	- Appropriate co-ordination of traffic signals on the adjacent urban streets
- Prevention of accidents on the motorway	- Signs for variable speed limits
	- Warning signs
	- Lane closure signs

Detection of:	Detection means
- volume - speed - occupancy - queues	- loop detectors

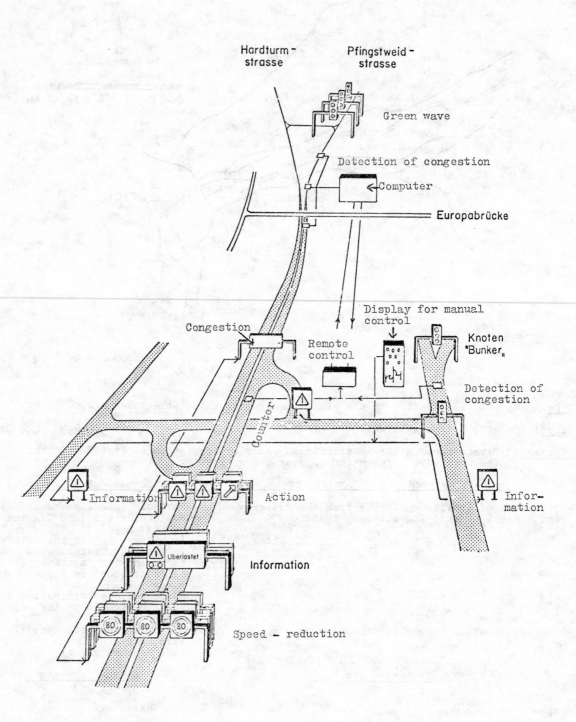

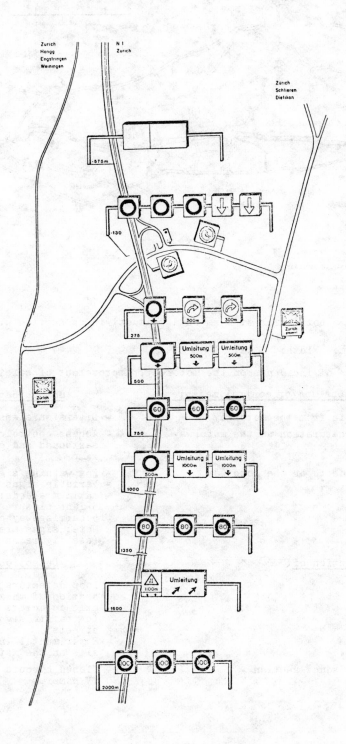

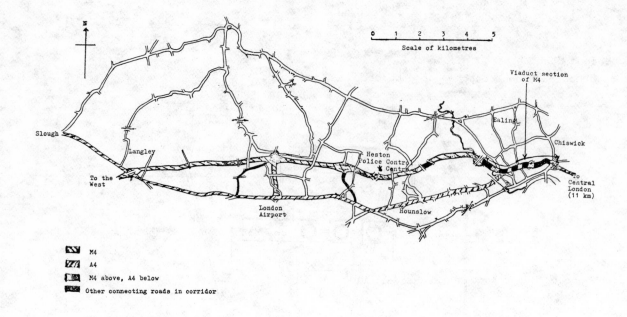

Type: Motorway (with a bottleneck at 4 km on a viaduct) in connection with parallel streets.

Scope: Length: 18 km. Width: 4 km.

Strategy: Prevention of incidents on the motorway, improvement of safety.

System functions and/or control measures	Communication means
- Diversion of traffic from the motorway	- Diversion signs at exit ramps
- Prevention of oversaturation on the motorway	- Access control signs on all eastbound and one westbound on-ramp
- Prevention of incidents on the motorway	- Fog warning signs on on-ramps - Variable signs giving 5 advisory maximum speeds; 5 lane closures (viaduct section) 5 carriageway closures Note: signs are of matrix type (see figure on next page)

Detection of:	Detection means
- Occupancy	- Loop detectors on viaduct section of the motorway
- Vehicle axles	- axle detectors on all approaches to traffic signals on adjacent streets
- Incidents	- Experimental incident detection site on the motorway
Observation of the viaduct section	- Closed circuit TV cameras

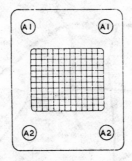

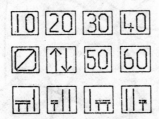

(a) Post-mounted carriageway signals

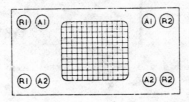

(b) Gantry-mounted lane signals

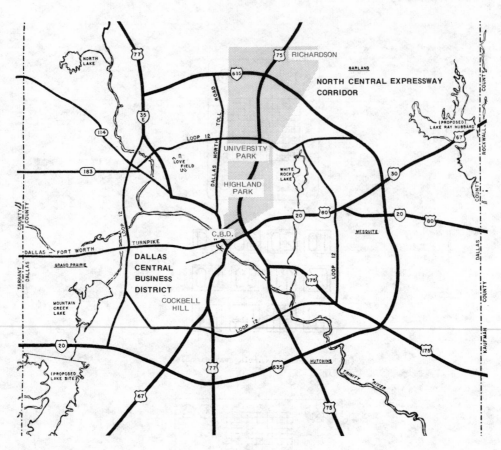

Type: Motorway with frontage roads and parallel arterials leading to the adjacent signal-controlled urban street network.

Scope: Length: 16 km.   Width: 5 km.

Strategy: Maximisation of throughput. Improvement of safety, priority to buses.

System functions and/or control measures

- Predictive information about traffic conditions on the motorway
- Prevention of oversaturation on the motorway and diversion of motorway traffic to the frontage roads or arterials

- Bus priority at motorway entrance and signal controlled intersection

Communication means

- Radio, variable message signs

- Ramp control signals. Variable signs for diversion of motorway traffic to frontage roads on arterials (see fig. on next page)
- Adequate co-ordination of traffic signals at the frontage roads and the street network
- Extension of green-times at ramp control and street signals for buses.

Detection of:

- Volume (flow-rate) ⎫
- Speed   ⎪
- Queues on the motorway ⎬
- Queues on the on-ramps ⎪
- Buses   ⎭

Detection means

- Loop detectors

- Special detectors

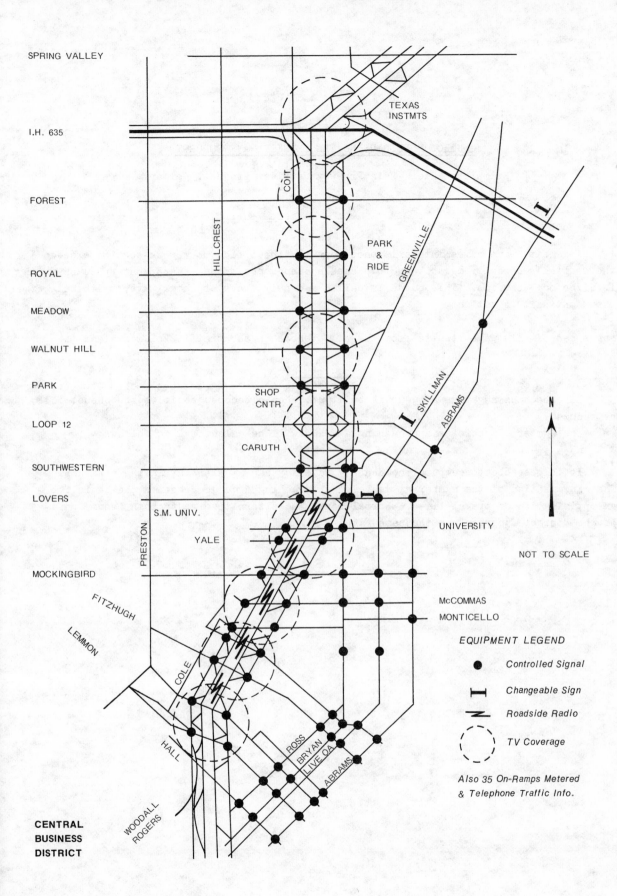

SPRING VALLEY

I.H. 635

TEXAS INSTMTS

COIT

FOREST

HILLCREST

PARK & RIDE

GREENVILLE

ROYAL

MEADOW

WALNUT HILL

PARK

SHOP CNTR

SKILLMAN

ABRAMS

LOOP 12

CARUTH

N

SOUTHWESTERN

LOVERS

S.M. UNIV.

PRESTON

YALE

UNIVERSITY

NOT TO SCALE

MOCKINGBIRD

FITZHUGH

McCOMMAS

MONTICELLO

LEMMON

EQUIPMENT LEGEND

● Controlled Signal

COLE

Changeable Sign

Roadside Radio

HALL

ROSS

BRYAN

LIVE OAK

ABRAMS

TV Coverage

Also 35 On-Ramps Metered & Telephone Traffic Info.

WOODALL ROGERS

CENTRAL BUSINESS DISTRICT

Annex 3

CONTROL MODELS USING THE DENSITY WAVE CONCEPT

Example of Rhein-Main Freeway Corridor Project, Germany

A density wave comes into existence when the input flow to a weak-section exceeds the section's capacity max q. In this case a queue occurs the development speed of which is directed backwards. This queue is called a density wave or shock wave. With help of the "continuity equation"

$$q = k \cdot v$$

the speed of this wave results from the differences in the traffic volumes q and the density k:

$$c = \frac{q - \max q}{k - \max k}$$

If c becomes negative a queue is built up, when c becomes positive the queue will be reduced.

The number of vehicles approaching a queue will be calculated as follows:
$$n_s = q - c \cdot k = \max q - c \cdot \max k$$

It is possible to compute the density wave for each weak point in the corridor. The minimisation of the number of vehicles approaching a queue presents the basis for an optimisation of travel times. Normal route and alternative route both become part of the "target function" at the same time.

Figure 1

EXAMPLE FOR «PARALLEL CORRIDOR»

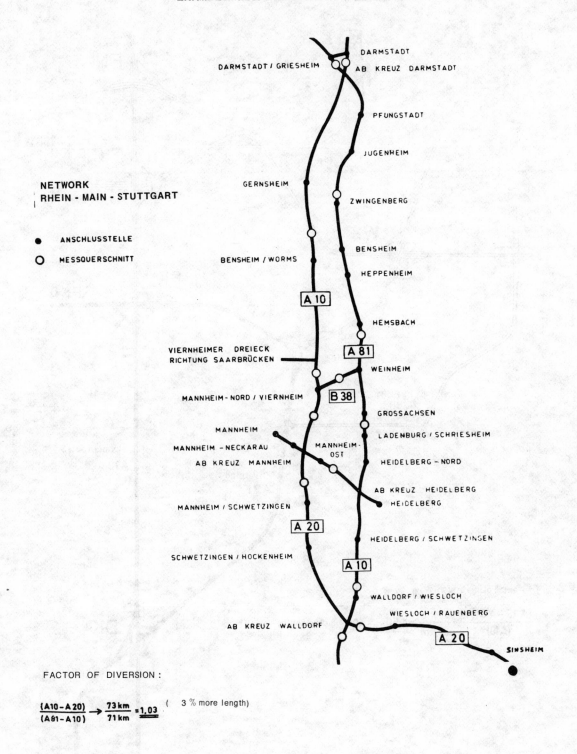

NETWORK
RHEIN - MAIN - STUTTGART

● ANSCHLUSSTELLE

○ MESSQUERSCHNITT

DARMSTADT

DARMSTADT / GRIESHEIM   AB KREUZ DARMSTADT

PFUNGSTADT

JUGENHEIM

GERNSHEIM

ZWINGENBERG

BENSHEIM

BENSHEIM / WORMS

HEPPENHEIM

A 10

HEMSBACH

A 81

VIERNHEIMER DREIECK
RICHTUNG SAARBRÜCKEN   WEINHEIM

MANNHEIM - NORD / VIERNHEIM   B 38

GROSSACHSEN

LADENBURG / SCHRIESHEIM

MANNHEIM

MANNHEIM - NECKARAU   MANNHEIM-
AB KREUZ MANNHEIM   OST   HEIDELBERG - NORD

AB KREUZ HEIDELBERG
HEIDELBERG

MANNHEIM / SCHWETZINGEN

A 20

HEIDELBERG / SCHWETZINGEN

SCHWETZINGEN / HOCKENHEIM   A 10

WALLDORF / WIESLOCH

WIESLOCH / RAUENBERG

AB KREUZ WALLDORF   A 20   SINSHEIM

FACTOR OF DIVERSION :

$$\frac{(A10 - A20)}{(A81 - A10)} \longrightarrow \frac{73\,km}{71\,km} = \underline{\underline{1.03}} \qquad (\quad 3\,\%\ more\ length)$$

Figure 2

EXAMPLE FOR «NOT-PARALLEL CORRIDOR»

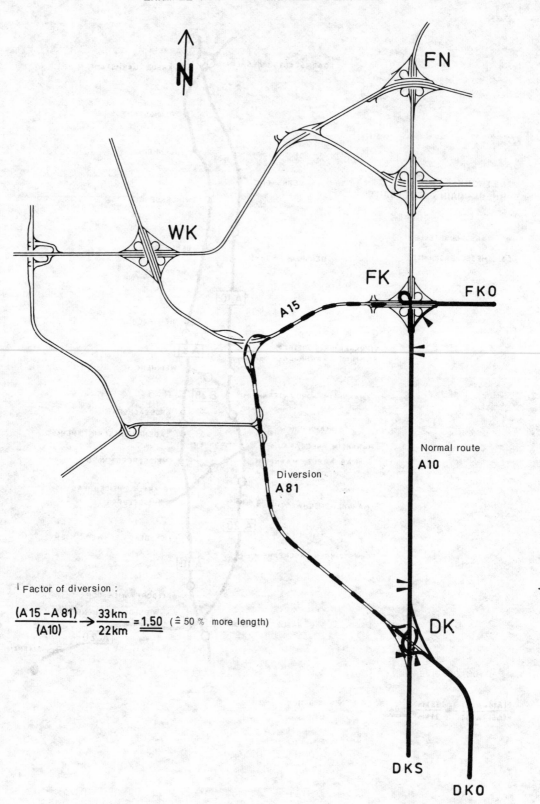

N

FN

WK

FK

FKO

A 15

Normal route
A 10

Diversion
A 81

Factor of diversion :

$$\frac{(A\,15 - A\,81)}{(A10)} \rightarrow \frac{33\,km}{22\,km} = \underline{\underline{1,50}} \; (\hat{=} \; 50 \, \% \; more \; length)$$

DK

DKS

DKO

Figure 3

EXAMPLE OF THREE O-D MATRICES

Mondays	7.00 - 10.00
Fridays	14.30 - 17.30
Sundays and holidays	14.30 - 17.30

to \ from	Friday			Sundays and holidays			Mondays		
	FN	DKO	DKS	FN	DKO	DKS	FN	DKO	DKS
FN	-	X	X	-	X	X	-	X	X
FK	-	X	X	-	X	X	-	X	X
DK	X	-	-	X	-	-	X	-	-
WK	-	X	X	-	X	X	-	X	X
MATRIX	1			2			3		

Figure 4
EXAMPLE OF RESULTS

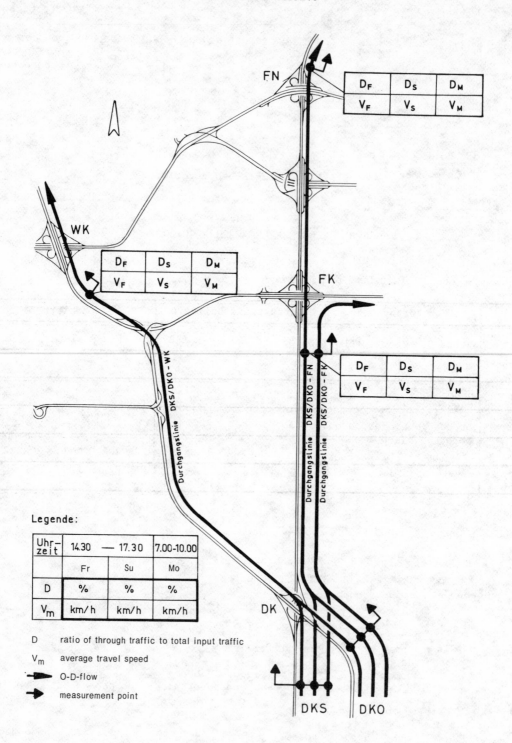

Annex 4

CONTROL MODELS USING THE CRITICAL QUEUE CONCEPT

Example of Dallas Freeway Corridor Project, U.S.A.

The expressway travel time is defined as normal travel time plus queue travel in the bottleneck section. Queue travel time is given by:

$$r_q = \frac{\text{number of vehicles in queue}}{\text{flow rate of bottleneck section}} = \frac{n_q}{s_q}$$

The "critical queue" is the minimum queue that warrants a diversion. A diversion is justified when the additional travel time, Δr, plus the normal travel time r_n, is at least equal to the travel time on the alternative route, r_{altern}, augmented by 50 per cent:

$$\Delta r + r_n \geqslant 1.5 r_{altern} = \text{critical travel time}$$

When Δr and r_q are equated - though this means a simplification - it is possible to compute the number of vehicles in the queue:

$$r_q = (1.5 r_{altern} - r_n) \cdot s_q$$

With a queue density of k vehicles per lane-mile and n_1 lanes, the length of the critical queue will be as follows:

$$l_q = \frac{n_q}{n_1 \cdot k}$$

For every weak point in a corridor the length of the critical queue can be determined and compared with the actual queue length. If the actual length of the queue exceeds the length of the critical queue a diversion will be justified.

Annex 5

CONTROL MODELS BASED ON LINEAR PROGRAMMING

Information on the Japanese and French works on linear programming

I. Tokyo expressway traffic control system

Principle of the short term prediction system (STPS)

STPS is a sort of a periodic scanning traffic simulation programme which simulates traffic condition of 30 minutes period starting from the initial condition which is calculated and filed in the data file by TCSS(1). The whole network of Tokyo Expressway can be simulated at one time.

The outline of the simulation technique is as follows:

a) the scanning interval is two to three minutes,

b) the whole network is divided into a number of links. A link is a stretch of road between merging or diverging points which are called nodes and have their own capacity constraints.

When an incident occurs, the incident becomes a temporary node.

c) traffic condition is expressed with three parameters as follows:

I_k (t) : accumulated input flow of the kth link at time t,

O_k (t) : accumulated output flow of the kth link at time t,

W_k (t) : number of vehicles present in the kth link at time t.

$$I_k (t) = O_{k-1} (t)$$

$$W_k (t) = I_k (t) - O_k (t) + W_k (0)$$

d) W_k (0) and traffic density or flow rate of each link should be given as the initial condition by TCSS,

e) I_k (t), O_k (t) and W_k (t) can be vectors if composition of various destinations is needed for determining diversion volumes but in the present STPS those parameters are not vectors. Instead, diverging ratio at a diverging point is expressed as a linear function of merging volumes at the nearest upstream major merging point.

f) Input flow prediction of an on-ramp is made based on the normalized historical flow pattern and its enlargement factor which is a function of the real volume in the last 30 minutes.

g) W_k (t) is controlled so as to follow the given flow-density relationship.

h) Travel times of the links in each scanning interval are calculated and tabulated.

---

1) Traffic condition surveillance system.

i) Positions of the tails of congested flows are also calculated according to the given flow density relationships.

Updating system

UDS is to update automatically the following various system parameters through study effects by means of exponential smoothing using the actually observed data.

a) On-ramp flow patterns,

b) diversion ratios,

c) merging ratios in congested conditions,

d) flow-density relationships,

e) flow differences between lanes,

f) speed differences between lanes,

(e and f in the above list are for detector performance examination carried out on line every minute by TCSS).

II. A6 B6 C6 motorway traffic control system

Principle of the programme used in the traffic control system of the motorway A6 B6 C6 (AFRODIT).

For a given network, for a given O-D matrix and for a given driver's response to the variable direction signs, AFRODIT gives the best signalling programme and the traffic flow to be admitted at each entrance of the network under the following conditions criterion: maximise the throughput with keeping a good level of service on the motorways - a secondary criterion like maximise the traffic flow of a particular entrance can also be used.

The programme itself is a "Branch and Bound - Simplex". The basic formulation of the programme is given below.

Notations:

$D_i \longrightarrow$ Traffic demand at the access i,

$D_{ij} \longrightarrow$ Traffic demand from i to j,

$Q_i \longrightarrow$ Traffic measured at the access i,

$Q_{ij} \longrightarrow$ Traffic flow going from i to j,

$Q_{ijk} \longrightarrow$ Traffic flow going from i to j by the k way (if there are several ways),

$x \longrightarrow$ Junction in the network,

$xy \longrightarrow$ Arc in the network,

$C_{(xy)} \longrightarrow$ Capacity of the arc xy,

$J_{(xy)} \longrightarrow$ Various ways using xy,

$K_i \longrightarrow \dfrac{Qi}{D_i} \quad (K_i \leqq 1)$

Formulation of the problem

$$\text{Max} \sum D_{ij} \cdot K_i \qquad (1)$$

$$0 \leqslant K_i \leqslant 1 \qquad (2)$$

$$\sum_{J(xy)} Q_{ijk} \leqslant C(xy) \qquad (3)$$

$$\sum_k Q_{ijk} - D_{ij} \cdot K_i = 0 \qquad (4)$$

The relation (1) is related to the criterion.

The relation (2), (3), (4) are conditions on traffic flows and capacities.

One can see here the typical formulation of a classical linear programme, the "K_i" and Q_{ijk} being the unknown values.

Annex 6

AUTOMATIC INCIDENT DETECTION MODEL BASED ON OCCUPANCY PARAMETERS

The model described here is used in the Naples Tollway Surveillance and Control System. In the system loop detectors are installed on a lane by lane basis every 250 m on the motorway and every 125 m inside tunnels. Every minute, n, average occupancy, O, is computed on every detector, i. Taking into consideration detector i, if the average occupancy is above the 8 per cent value, the following expression is computed

$$D_s = \frac{O_{n,i} - O_{n,i+1}}{O_{n,i}} \qquad (1)$$

where $O_{n,i}$ = average occupancy at minute n on detector i

$O_{n,i+1}$ = average occupancy at minute n on detector i+1, the downstream detector on the same lane.

If D_s is larger than a given threshold the presence of a traffic "space discontinuity" is detected.

At the same time the following expression is computed

$$D_t = \frac{O_{n,i} - O_{n-1,i}}{O_{n-1,i}} \qquad (2)$$

where $O_{n-1,i}$ = average occupancy at minute n-1 on detector i.

This second test is a "time" test which detects the passage of the "shock wave" (time discontinuity) over the detector. If D_t is larger than a given threshold the possible presence of an incident is assumed. At the following minute the test (1) is repeated and if the threshold is exceeded again (meaning that the discontinuity is of a stable type) the incident is confirmed and assumed as detected.

The end of an incident is determined when D_s is under the given threshold (equalisation of parameter along the traffic lane).

Annex 7

STATISTICAL INFORMATION ON MOTORWAY CLOSURES IN ENGLAND

An examination of the policies and procedures followed by three police authorities in respect of incidents which involve closure of motorway carriageways shows that for short period closures the authorities consider it preferable to hold traffic on the motorway. Only for expected closures of over an hour (and even longer where the adjoining road network is unsuitable or overloaded) is diversion contemplated or the possibility considered of arranging two-way working on the remaining carriageway. In order to check the practical effects of this policy an analysis was undertaken of motorway closures over a 12 month period (November 1972 to October 1973) in order to obtain the distribution of closure times. The results are tabulated in Table 1. At the end of the survey period there was approximately 1500 route kilometres of motorway in operation (3000 km. of carriageway). Approximately 87.5 per cent of the network is dual 3-lane, the remainder being dual 2-lane. Of 115 closures during this period the duration in respect of half of the incidents is 85 minutes or less, whilst the average duration of closure is 150 minutes. The further breakdown of figures shows that the number of closures per annum per hundred kilometres of carriageway for 3-lane motorways is between 4 and 5, whilst on 2-lane motorways (excluding the non-typical viaduct lengths of M4 on the Western approach to London) the closure rate is some 2 or 3 times higher. This greater incidence of closure on 2-lane motorways can mean that problems of closure are significantly greater in those countries where the proportion of 2-lane motorways is higher. It may also be worth noting that about 1 in 10 of all closures affected both carriageways, thereby causing total motorway closure with all the added problems that this entails.

ANALYSIS OF MOTORWAY CARRIAGEWAY CLOSURES. 12 MONTH
(Nov. 1972 - Oct. 1973 inc.)

Total carriageway closures = 115*

Average duration of closure ≈ 150 mins

Half total closures 85 mins or less

* excludes closure resulting from damaged
  overbridge which took over 2 days

a → Also 2 Closures 650 mins
          2 Closures 725 mins
          2 Closures 910 mins

No. of closures

Durée (mn)
Duration (mins)

TYPES OF VARIABLE MESSAGE SIGNS

	PRINCIPLE OF OPERATION	TYPICAL DIMENSIONS	NUMBER OF POSSIBLE DISPLAYS	MINIMUM TIME NEEDED TO CHANGE MESSAGE	NOTES
ROTATABLE LAMINAE	Set of revolving laminae rotatable about an axis and controlling by electromagnets (airport types).	1.1m x 1.1m	2 – 30	3 sec	• size limited by degree of flexibility of laminae • this type still poses practical problems in field applications
PRISMS	Set of one or several prisms revolving about a horizontal axis; selection of static positions with limit-switch indexing.	0.7m x 7m (maximum)	3-4; multiple prism system ≤10; single prism system	1.5 sec	• illumination from an internal source • number of displays is limited
SCROLL	Strip in translucent synthetic material; feed and takeup spools mounted at either end of panel. Indexing by photocell or detector.	1.1m x 1.1m	≤ 30	1.5 sec	• rearside illumination • high quality strip material necessary to preclude sticking after prolonged periods of non-operation
CONTINUED STRIPS	Similar to scroll; except that the strip is a continuous loop and a given display can be obtained by moving the strip in either direction.	1.1m x 1.1m	2 - 3	1.4 sec	• similar to scroll • can be operated vertically or horizontally
ROLLERS	Set of panels of flexible material, wrapped around individual rollers. Panel selection is affected by roller selection.	1.1m x 1.1m	~10	4 sec	• similar to scroll • visibility of the panels depends on their position in the container
ROLLERS ON CONTINUOUS BELT	Similar to rollers; however the rollers are mounted on a continuous belt so that the roller chosen can be located as desired.	1.1m x 1.1m	≤10		• similar to scroll • chosen panel is always located in the best position, i.e. at the front
SLIDING PANELS	Assembly consists of two sections: a closed compartment for panel storage and another compartment with an open face which receives the selected panel	1.5m x 1.5m	6 or 10	2 sec	• sliding mechanism can cause problems • provides good visibility • rearside illumination • system can consist of half panels stored in separate compartments
LIGHT MATRIX	Set of lamps forming a display of n lines and m columns. Selective lamp illumination enables display of different symbols or characters. (It is also possible to use fibre glass cables that direct light from a central light source to different panel sections).	Variable	Unlimited	Instant	• excellent operational flexibility • cannot form directional messages conforming to the Vienna Int'l Sign Convention

1. ROTATABLE LAMINAE

2. PRISMS

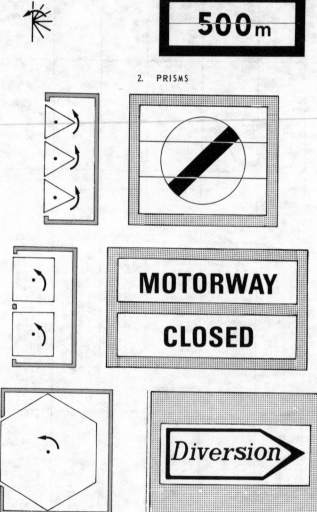

3. SCROLL

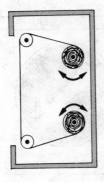 

4. CONTINUOUS STRIP

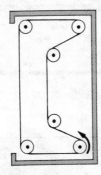 

5. ROLLERS

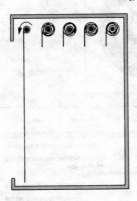 

6. ROLLERS ON CONTINUOUS BELT

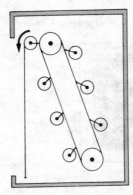 

7. SLIDING PANELS

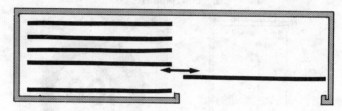

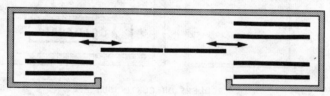

8. MATRIX OF LAMPS

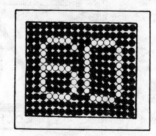

LIST OF MEMBERS OF THE GROUP

Chairman:	Dr. W. Wolman, United States
Vice Chairmen:	Mr. M. Halpern Herla, France
	Dr. K. Krell, Germany

BELGIUM
BELGIQUE

Dr. L. de Brabander
Fonds d'Etudes et de Recherches pour la
Sécurité Routière
14 rue du Gouvernement Provisoire
Bruxelles 100

FRANCE

Mr. Halpern Herla
Institut de Recherche sur les Transports
Avenue du Général Malleret-Joinville
94 - Arcueil

Mr. Jean-Paul Le Cocq
S.E.T.R.A.
46 Avenue A. Briand
92223 Bagneux

Mr. Michel Ledru
S.E.T.R.A.
46 avenue A. Briand
92223 Bagneux

GERMANY
ALLEMAGNE

Mr. Boesefeldt
Beratende Ingenieure
51 Aachen
Peterstrasse 2-4

Mr. K. Everts
Consulting Engineer
Heusch-Boesefeldt
51 Aachen
Peterstrasse 2-4

Prof. Dr. K. Krell
Bundesanstalt für Strassenwesen
5 Köln 51
Brühlerstrasse 1

ITALY
ITALIE

Prof. Dr. Roberto Vacca
CGA
20 via Fumaroli
Roma

JAPAN
JAPON

Mr. A. Ishido
Ministry of Construction, Public Works
Research Institute, Chiba Branch,
12-52 Anagawa 4,
Chibashi,
Chibaken

Mr. Toshihiro Kikuta
Tokyo Metropolitan Expressway Public Corporation
1-4-1 Kasumigaseki
Chiyoda-ku
Tokyo

Dr. Masaki Koshi
University of Tokyo
7-22 1 Rappongi
Minatoku
Tokyo

LUXEMBURG
LUXEMBOURG

Mr. A. Millim
Direction de la Police
Case Postale 242
5 rue Auguste Lumière
Luxembourg

NETHERLANDS
PAYS BAS

Mr. B. de Hoop
Ministry of Transport
Traffic Engineering Division
Koningskade 4
The Hague

Mr. Klijnhout
Rykswaterstaat
Koningskade 4
The Hague

SPAIN
ESPAGNE

M. M. Gullon Low
Direccion General de Carreteras
Ministerio de Obras Publicas
P. Castellana
Madrid

M. F. Mir-Espinet
Chief Engineer of Traffic Department
Marco Aurelio 1
Barcelona

SWEDEN
SUEDE

Mr. Karl Bang
VBB Consulting Engineers
Geijersgatan 8
21618 Malmö

SWITZERLAND
SUISSE

M. Marcel Jenni
Jenni & Voorhees AG
Hutschellenstrasse 21
CH - 8002 Zürich

M. A. Spring
Stv. Stadtplaner
Stadtplanungsamt
Postfach 2731
3001 Bern

UNITED KINGDOM
ROYAUME UNI

Mr. B. Cobbe
Department of the Environment
Traffic Control and Communications Division
St. Christopher House
Southwark Street
London, S.E.1.

Mr. J.A. Hillier
Transport and Road Research Laboratory
Old Workingham Road
Crowthorne
Berkshire

Dr. J. Holroyd
Transport and Road Research Laboratory
Old Workingham Road
Crowthorne
Berkshire

<u>UNITED STATES</u>
<u>ETATS UNIS</u>

Dr. W. Wolman
Chief, Traffic Systems Division
Office of Research
Federal Highway Administration
U.S. Department of Transportation
<u>Washington D.C.</u> 20591

<u>OECD SECRETARIAT</u>

Mr. B. Horn

ABSTRACT

The OECD Group "International Corridor Experiment" (ICE-Project) was created to examine the strategies available for traffic corridor control and to outline potential international co-ordinated research that could be performed on a corridor facility of a Member country on the basis of the needs of another Member country. The Group's objective was to bring together and exploit the expertise on traffic control available in participating OECD countries in order to make the most rapid and efficient impact on the very complex subject of traffic corridor control. The experience of developments such as ramp control systems in the United States, co-ordinated signal control in Europe, and motorist warning systems in Japan provided the basis for the Group's work.

The following five types of corridors, both in urban and in rural areas (intra-city and inter-city), were considered within the framework of the programme:

1. Motorway and motorway;
2. Motorway and co-ordinated area traffic control system;
3. Motorway and street network (unco-ordinated control);
4. Motorway and suburban road network (including controlled arterials);
5. Motorway and rural roads.

The report contains six chapters, a list of key references and eight annexes. The Introduction describes the origins of the Group and highlights its accomplishments. Chapter II defines the objectives and criteria of traffic corridor control as well as the means for realising these objectives.

Chapter III presents a review of traffic corridor control concepts. In the first section a summary description of a corridor system is given showing the various components. The second section deals with control strategies subdivided into network control, ramp control and linear (speed and lane) control and three annexes present detailed information on some control models used in corridor facilities in operation. The third section provides an account of the most recent developments with regard to traffic incident management systems. The fourth section gives a short review of the principal hardware aspects (including an annex on variable message signs) and the fifth section examines the problem of driver response.

Chapter IV is devoted to the assessment of the total system. The assessment procedures include the evaluation of recurring, non-recurring and environmental problems, the analysis of the solutions with regard to the applicability of the various control strategies described in Chapter III, and the documentation of results so as to determine how well the system objectives are met. Chapter V discusses the approaches to economic evaluation and presents some practical examples. Chapter VI provides an outline of the main priority research areas: incident management; short-term prediction; strategies; assessment methods; driver communication techniques. A detailed inventory and description of the experimental corridor facilities included in the ICE Project is presented in an annex.

LIST OF PUBLICATIONS OF THE ROAD RESEARCH PROGRAMME

Road Traffic and Urban Transport

Electronic aids for freeway operation (April 1971)

Area traffic control systems (February 1972)

Optimisation of bus operation in urban areas (May 1972)

Two lane rural roads: road design and traffic flow (July 1972)

Traffic operation at sites of temporary obstruction (February 1973)

Effects of traffic and roads on the environment in urban areas (July 1973)

Proceedings of the symposium on techniques of improving urban conditions by restraint of road traffic (September 1973)

Urban traffic models: possibilities for simplification (August 1974)

Capacity of at-grade junctions (November 1974)

Proceedings of the symposium on roads and the urban environment (August 1975)

Road Safety

Alcohol and drugs (January 1968)

Pedestrian safety (October 1969)

Driver behaviour (June 1970)

Proceedings of the symposium on the use of statistical methods in the analysis of road accidents (September 1970)

Lighting, visibility and accidents (March 1971)

Research into road safety at junctions in urban areas (October 1971)

Road safety campaigns: design and evaluation (December 1971)

Speed limits outside built-up areas (August 1972)

Research on traffic law enforcement (April 1974)

Young driver accidents (March 1975)

Roadside obstacles (August 1975)

Manual on road safety campaigns (September 1975)

Road Construction and Maintenance

Research on crash barriers (February 1969)

Motor vehicle corrosion and influence of de-icing chemicals (October 1969)

Winter damage to road pavements (May 1972)

Accelerated methods of life-testing pavements (May 1972)

Proceedings of the symposium on the quality control of road works (July 1972)

Waterproofing of concrete bridge decks (July 1972)

Optimisation of road alignment by the use of computers (July 1973)

Water in roads: prediction of moisture content in road subgrades (August 1973)

Maintenance of rural roads (August 1973)

Water in roads: methods for determining soil moisture content and pore water tension (December 1973)

Proceedings of the Symposium on frost action on roads (October 1974)

Road marking and delineation (February 1975)

Resistance of flexible pavements to plastic deformation (May 1975)